The AI Playbook

The AI Playbook

Elias Trent

WTF is AI? (And Why Should You Care?)

L et's be honest: half the world is pretending to understand AI, and the other half is hoping it just goes away so we can get back to arguing about oat milk. But here's the problem — AI isn't going anywhere. In fact, it's already quietly taken over your life while you were busy Googling how to get rid of cookie pop-ups.

AI is everywhere now. It writes your YouTube captions, picks the next show you binge, filters your emails, and helps your phone recognize your face when you're still half asleep. And recently, it got a major upgrade — one that went from "useful" to "terrifyingly competent." Suddenly, AI can talk, write, draw, solve problems, explain quantum physics, or write bedtime stories about zombie unicorns in the voice of Morgan Freeman.

So what the hell is it?

In human-speak, AI is a computer system that mimics smart behavior — not because it's thinking like you, but because it's seen enough examples to fake it like a pro. Imagine someone who's read the entire internet, memorized it, and now just blurts out the most statistically likely thing to say next. That's pretty much it. It's not conscious. It doesn't understand you. But it's so good at mimicking us that it can pass for human, especially in corporate emails and tech blog comments.

Most of what we call "AI" today is just fancy prediction. You give it a sentence, it predicts the next word. You show it a blurry picture of your dog, it guesses what breed it is. You type "how to quit my job professionally," and it gives you a five-paragraph essay that sounds better than anything you've written sober.

Now, here's where things get spicy.

This stuff used to be trapped in the dungeons of big tech labs and nerd forums. But thanks to a few open releases — like ChatGPT — it got out. Now regular people (yes, even the ones who still use "password123") can use AI to write, design, research, automate, and even create music. That's why everyone from job recruiters to Instagram artists are either using it or nervously pretending they aren't.

And you should care. Not because the robots are coming to kill us — though they might someday — but because someone who does use AI can already do your job faster, cheaper, and without needing coffee breaks. And if they're using AI and you're not? Well, let's just say the company Christmas party's going to feel awkward when your replacement is a laptop with better posture than you.

The point isn't to fear this stuff. The point is to learn how to use it before you're forced to. This book will teach you exactly that — no jargon, no math, no weird tech cult vibes. Just real tools, real talk, and maybe a few jokes about Elon Musk.

You don't need to become a robot. You just need to learn how to work with them — and maybe even make them work for you.

Let's get to it.

Now let's clear something up before the next guy in a fleece vest corners you at a networking event. People throw around words like "AI," "machine learning," and "automation" like they're all the same thing. They're not. And most of the time, the person saying them doesn't actually know what they mean either. So here's the real breakdown — minus the jargon, and with all the BS surgically removed.

AI, as we've covered, is the broad concept: teaching computers to do stuff that usually requires a human brain. Thinking, speaking, recognizing patterns, all that jazz. When people say "AI is taking over," they're talking about this big umbrella idea — often without realizing the umbrella is full of holes and being held by a guy who still uses Internet Explorer.

Machine learning is what makes modern AI actually work. It's not programmed like a set of instructions. Instead, you feed it a ton of examples — data, images, language, whatever — and it figures out patterns on its own. It's like raising a child, if your child could absorb a billion textbooks overnight and never ask "are we there yet?"

Automation, on the other hand, is the more boring cousin. This is the stuff that follows rules: "If this, then that." Like your email app automatically sending that "I'm out of office and probably drinking" message. Automation doesn't think. It just does. Efficiently. Coldly. Like your least favorite coworker.

And finally, BS — the marketing fluff, buzzwords, and empty hype designed to sell you a "revolutionary" AI-powered toothbrush that tracks your gum health and sends push notifications you'll ignore. BS is everywhere in this space. It's what turns "basic script automation" into "cutting-edge AI workflow orchestration." Same thing. Fancier suit.

So when someone tells you they're "leveraging machine learning in an AI-enabled automation pipeline," what they probably mean is: "I connected a chatbot to a spreadsheet and now I charge consulting fees."

You don't need to become an expert in any of this — you just need to smell the difference between what's useful and what's hot air. And that's exactly what we're doing here.

You've probably been using AI for years without even knowing it — like how you didn't realize your phone was autocorrecting "duck" to something far less satisfying for your entire adult life.

When Netflix recommends that oddly specific Korean zombie dating show and you think, "How did it know?" — that's AI. When Gmail finishes your sentence for you — also AI. When Spotify makes a playlist that weirdly fits your mood even though you're going through a "maybe I'll move to the woods and raise goats" phase — you guessed it: AI. Your phone unlocking with your face?

AI.

Google Maps rerouting you mid-drive because traffic ahead looks like Mad Max?

Also AI.

Instagram showing you an ad for hiking boots five minutes after you thought about hiking but didn't even say anything out loud?

Probably AI... or the NSA. Who knows.

Point is, this stuff is already baked into your life. Quietly. Invisibly. And for the most part, it's been doing basic tasks: filtering spam, tagging your dog in photos, helping you avoid exes on Facebook memories. But now, those tools are getting way more powerful — and way more public.

The AI you're about to learn to use isn't just hiding behind your apps anymore. It's in your browser. It's in your work tools. It's in your kid's homework. And if you're not the one driving, you're riding shotgun while a bunch of bots take the wheel.

That's not fear-mongering — that's your Tuesday. You're already using AI. This book just shows you how to actually take control of it.

Let's get one thing straight: AI isn't a tech trend like NFTs, Clubhouse, or whatever cryptocurrency your cousin lost money on. This isn't a fad. It's more like... electricity.

When electricity showed up in the 1800s, people thought it was neat. Some fancy rich guy lit a lightbulb, everyone clapped, and nobody had any idea how much it would change everything. But over time, it crept into homes, factories, cities. It didn't just make life more convenient — it rewired civilization. Literally.

Same thing's happening now with AI.

Right now, people are oohing and aahing at chatbots writing poetry and image generators making Pope Francis look like he models for Balenciaga. Funny, yes. Useful, sometimes. But this is just the flickering lightbulb phase. What comes next is full-on infrastructure-level change. It's not just a tool you use — it becomes the foundation of how everything works.

Jobs, education, health care, logistics, media, finance — it's all getting rewritten, not with electricity this time, but with code that learns. Every industry, every system that involves patterns, data, or language is being quietly pulled into the AI slipstream.

And just like electricity, most people won't even notice it's there — until they lose access to it, or until someone else uses it better than them.

So no, this isn't another tech bubble. It's not a gimmick. It's not going to disappear when the hype cools down. It's going to melt into the background of modern life, just like Wi-Fi and complaining about gas prices. The only question left is:

Will you be one of the people using AI to power your work, ideas, and life — or one of the people left squinting in the dark, wondering what happened?

2

Will a Robot Take My Job?

L et's rip the Band-Aid off:
For the first time in human history, it's not the factory worker who's most at risk. It's the guy in khakis with a laptop and a LinkedIn bio full of vague verbs like "synergize" and "leverage."

Yes, I'm talking about white-collar work — the kind of jobs that have historically felt "safe," "prestigious," and "too complex" to be replaced by machines. The cubicle crowd. The Zoom warriors. The spreadsheet sorcerers and PowerPoint paladins. If your job involves emails, meetings, writing, data, or pretending to look busy while secretly checking Reddit, congratulations: you are now officially replaceable — or at least partially automatable.

This isn't fearmongering. It's what's already happening.

Copywriters? ChatGPT can write decent ad copy in seconds — and it doesn't charge for coffee breaks or ping your manager about "creative differences."

Paralegals? There are legal AI tools that can read 200 contracts while you're still figuring out which PDF has the correct font.

Journalists? Some news outlets are already publishing AI-written stories with fewer typos and less existential dread.

Middle managers? AI is shockingly good at summarizing meetings, assigning tasks, and sending passive-aggressive follow-up emails. (Honestly, maybe too good.)

Even programmers — the sacred priesthood of the tech world — are being assisted, outpaced, and in some cases, sidelined by code-generating bots that work 24/7 and don't argue about tabs vs. spaces.

Here's the uncomfortable truth:

If your job is mostly thinking, typing, and talking — AI can probably do at least part of it faster and cheaper.

This isn't some future scenario. This is now. Companies are already trimming teams and replacing "knowledge workers" with tools that don't complain, unionize, or ask for ergonomic chairs.

And yet — this isn't a death sentence.

Because here's the catch: AI is incredibly powerful, but it's still dumb in all the ways that matter most. It has no judgment, no taste, no emotional intelligence, and no clue how to navigate nuance unless you spoon-feed it instructions. It can summarize a Zoom call, but it can't negotiate a raise. It can write a press release, but it can't decide whether your company should launch that product in the first place. It can draft ideas — but you still have to know which ones are crap.

The people who are really at risk aren't the ones who use AI. It's the ones who pretend it doesn't matter. Or worse, who believe their job is too sacred, too human, or too creative to ever be threatened by "just a tool."

Sound familiar? That's exactly what taxi drivers said about Uber.

Exactly what Blockbuster said about Netflix.

Exactly what travel agents said before we all started booking flights in our pajamas while half-asleep.

History is brutal to the comfortable. And right now, comfort is a luxury most professionals can't afford.

But you don't need to panic. You need to pivot.

The good news? You're already doing that. You're reading this book. You're asking questions. You're thinking about your role in the new economy, and you're smart enough to want to stay ahead of it instead of praying it passes you by.

And that's the difference between getting replaced — and becoming irreplaceable.

Now that we've established that your job might be standing a little too close to the ledge, let's talk about who's actually in danger — and who's still got some solid footing (for now).

First, the sitting ducks.

If your job involves moving information from one place to another, summarizing things, writing generic content, or repeating the same task over and over, you're in the danger zone. Not because you're bad at what you do, but because machines have become terrifyingly good at mimicking that kind of work.

Here's a rough breakdown of jobs most at risk:

• Administrative assistants – AI can already schedule meetings, summarize emails, and generate reports. And it doesn't mind Karen from accounting.

• Customer service reps – Chatbots don't need breaks, don't take sick days, and never get snarky (unless you ask them to).

• Data entry clerks – AIs don't fat-finger spreadsheet columns, and they can process thousands of records faster than your best caffeine-fueled day.

• Junior copywriters & content marketers – If your job is writing "10 tips for better sleep" blogs, AI can crank those out before you've opened your doc.

• Paralegals, analysts, low-level coders – The workhorses of document-heavy and rule-based fields are being augmented — or in some cases, quietly sidelined — by software that doesn't need a salary or a law degree.

Even creative jobs aren't immune. AI can now generate logos, compose music, design websites, and even help script entire videos. It's not always great, but it's often good enough — and for a lot of businesses, good enough for half the cost is a very tempting deal.

But don't despair. Some roles are still relatively safe — especially the ones that require human complexity, personal interaction, or ethical judgment. These jobs rely on things AI still sucks at: empathy, originality, leadership, and intuition.

Here are some of the more protected categories — at least for now:

- Skilled trades – Plumbers, electricians, welders, mechanics. Unless we invent a robot that can crawl under your sink and improvise with rusty pipes, these jobs are sticking around.
- Therapists, social workers, coaches – Empathy can't be faked (not well), and no AI can truly hold space for someone's pain — or offer advice with real soul.
- Strategists, leaders, entrepreneurs – The people making high-level decisions, taking risks, and reading between the lines still have the edge... if they use AI as a tool, not a crutch.
- Artists with taste – AI can generate images. But knowing what's good? What's cool? What resonates? That's still a human game — at least until robots start having midlife crises and ironic mustaches.
- Hands-on caregivers – Nurses, early childhood educators, and people who do the deeply personal work of helping other people survive and thrive — AI can't hold a hand, change a diaper, or talk a kid down from a tantrum. Yet.

The bottom line?

If your work is soul-less, it's replaceable. If your work has soul — and you're adaptable — you've got leverage.

That doesn't mean you're totally safe. No one is. But it means the key to surviving (and thriving) in this new economy is knowing what you bring to the table that a robot can't fake — and then supercharging it with the right tools.

Which brings us to the next question:

What exactly makes a human irreplaceable?

Okay, so you've seen the warning signs. You're watching the bots get faster, cheaper, and weirdly good at writing press releases. Your job, or at least parts of it, is under siege. But you're not doomed — you're early. And being early means you've got a head start.

So let's talk defense. And more importantly, let's talk offense.

Here's how to AI-proof your career in a world where machines are learning to talk, think, and maybe even flirt better than your coworkers.

1. Stop Competing With AI — Start Collaborating With It

If you're doing tasks that a bot can now handle, don't fight it. Don't dig in. Don't say, "Well I prefer to do it the old-fashioned way." That's how Blockbuster felt about Netflix. Where's Blockbuster now?

Instead, use AI to augment what you do. Use it to brainstorm, draft, edit, summarize, automate, analyze. Become the AI-powered version of you — the one who delivers the same value in half the time with ten times the insight.

You don't need to be replaced by a robot if you become the human using one.

2. Double Down on the Skills AI Can't Fake (Yet)

AI is fast. But it's dumb about certain things. If you want to stay ahead, build the muscles it doesn't have:

• Judgment — knowing why something matters, not just what it is.
• Taste — knowing the difference between decent and extraordinary.
• Empathy — understanding people in a way data never will.
• Curiosity — asking better questions, not just finding faster answers.
• Adaptability — updating yourself faster than the tech does.

In short: get weirder, more human, more multidimensional. The cookie-cutter roles will be cut first. Be the one no template can replace.

3. Don't Just Do the Work — Own the Workflow

AI isn't going to kill your job. But the person who knows how to build an AI-powered workflow might.

So stop thinking in tasks. Start thinking in systems.

Can you automate the routine parts of your work? Can you build a process others rely on? Can you become the person who makes things more efficient — not just the one following instructions?

Own the tools. Run the systems. Be the one other people go to when they realize the robots are coming for them.

4. Build a Reputation, Not Just a Résumé

The resume is dying. Your brand is not.

In an AI-saturated world, your perspective, voice, and personal credibility matter more than ever. AI can write content — but you can write with authority. AI can summarize research — but you can show up in a meeting and explain what it actually means.

If you build trust, show your work, and have an opinion worth hearing, you'll stand out no matter how many bots flood the market. You'll become uncopyable — which is the new untouchable.

Start a blog. Post insights. Give value. Build a body of work that screams, "This person gets it — and we can't replace that with an app."

5. Learn How to Learn (Like a Machine)

You don't need to know everything — you just need to know how to learn anything, fast.

The best thing you can do right now? Develop the skill of rapid up-skilling. Learn the tools. Try the platforms. Break them. Watch tutorials. Ask questions. Mess around. Iterate. Move.

Because while everyone else is still arguing over whether AI is a threat or a trend, you'll be doing what matters most: learning how to surf the wave instead of getting flattened by it.

The truth is, there's no such thing as permanent job security anymore. But there's something better: career adaptability.

The people who succeed in the AI age won't be the ones who know everything.

They'll be the ones who keep evolving.

So stop asking, "Will I get replaced?"

Start asking, "How do I become too valuable to ignore — with or without AI?"

Spoiler: that's what we'll help you do in the next chapter.

Let's be real: you're not going to outwork a machine. It doesn't sleep, doesn't snack, doesn't get distracted by YouTube rabbit holes. You're also not going to out-remember it. It's been trained on the entire internet — good luck competing with that on trivia night.

But here's where you win: you can do what it can't.

You can synthesize ideas from opposite worlds. You can connect dots it doesn't even see. You can feel, imagine, question, rebel. You can turn chaos into meaning, raw data into purpose, and mistakes into breakthroughs. The machine can write the sentence. But only you can write the truth.

So no — the future doesn't belong to pure AI. And it definitely doesn't belong to people still pretending AI is just a fad.

It belongs to the hybrids.

The ones who know how to think like humans, and operate like machines.

The ones who wield AI like a weapon — not fear it like a ghost.

The ones who combine instinct with tools, wisdom with speed, creativity with code.

Think of it like this:

If old-school workers are horses, and AI is a car, the hybrid is a cyborg driving the car while building a spaceship in the backseat.

Hybrids don't just keep their jobs — they rewrite them.

They don't wait to be disrupted — they disrupt themselves first.

They don't follow AI — they lead it. Train it. Shape it.

And they're not rare unicorns. They're ordinary people who made a simple decision:

To stop fighting the future, and start upgrading themselves.

You don't need to become a machine.

You just need to stop working like one.

In the chapters ahead, we'll show you how to do exactly that — how to pick up the tools, plug them into your brain, and become the kind of worker, thinker, and creator that can't be replaced. Because once you unlock that? You're not just surviving the AI age. You're dominating it. Let's get to work.

3

AI: Tool, Tyrant, or Teammate?

Big Tech's Agenda vs. Your Freedom
Let's get something uncomfortable out of the way.

Yes, AI is powerful. Yes, it's revolutionary. And yes, it can absolutely make your life easier, faster, and possibly more lucrative.

But let's not pretend this is all sunshine, unicorns, and benevolent robot butlers handing you productivity on a silver platter. The people building this stuff aren't just doing it to "help humanity." They're doing it to control markets, shape behavior, and cash in — big time.

The current AI boom isn't some grassroots utopia. It's being driven by a handful of tech giants who didn't suddenly grow a conscience. These are the same companies that already control your emails, your search results, your news feeds, your shopping habits, your attention span, and maybe your thermostat. They didn't lose sleep over your privacy back when they were just selling ads — and they're not likely to start now that they've built something that can imitate your writing style and talk like your dead grandmother.

So while the headlines say "AI is the future," what they usually mean is: "We're the future — and you're the product."

You don't have to be a conspiracy theorist to see it. Just follow the money. The big players want AI to be powerful, but not necessarily open. They want it to be helpful, but only if it keeps you on their platform. They want it to "democratize" knowledge, sure — but under their terms of service.

And if you're not careful, it's easy to get sucked in.

Use their tools, follow their prompts, rely on their systems... and before long, you're not just using AI. You're dependent on it. You stop thinking for yourself because the machine spits out answers faster than your brain can question them. You trust it. You defer to it. You don't notice the invisible hands shaping the data behind the curtain.

And this is where it gets tricky.

Because AI isn't evil. It's not inherently manipulative or biased.

But the people who train it — and the systems that monetize it — absolutely can be. And often are.

So how do you stay free in a world where the most powerful tools are owned by the least trustworthy corporations?

You own your relationship to the tech.

You question the outputs, not just consume them.

You learn how the sausage is made, even if you're not the one coding it.

You don't surrender your thinking to convenience. You don't outsource your values. You stay human — and in control — even when the machine starts sounding smarter than your boss.

Because AI can be a tool.

It can even be a teammate.

But the second you forget who's holding the leash, you become the tool.

And that's not the future we're building here.

Let's say you hand over a few small tasks to AI. No big deal, right?

First it's your emails. Then your to-do list. Then your decisions. Then your voice.

Suddenly, the only thing left doing the actual thinking is a black box filled with autocomplete suggestions and corporate guardrails.

That's what giving up your agency looks like.

It doesn't happen all at once. It's slow. Comfortable. Convenient.

Until one day, you realize you've outsourced not just your work, but your will.

The danger isn't just that AI will do things for you.

It's that it will start deciding what gets done, why, and how you should feel about it.

When you let AI — especially Big Tech's AI — run your day, write your thoughts, schedule your time, answer your messages, summarize your meetings, and suggest your content, you start living in a reality curated for you by a machine trained on everyone else's noise.

You stop choosing. You start reacting.

You stop discerning. You start agreeing.

You stop creating. You start approving.

And that's when you become exactly what these systems want:

Predictable. Passive. Contained.

Because the truth is, AI systems don't just want to be helpful.

They want you hooked. They're designed — literally engineered — to optimize for engagement, conformity, and ease.

And you? You're human. You're tired. You're busy. You take the short-cut.

But shortcuts come with a toll.

When you stop thinking critically, you get more output — but less insight.

When you stop struggling, you get more speed — but less growth.

When you stop editing, doubting, questioning, and revising, you get more content — but less character.

And what's left?

A world where everything sounds smart but means nothing. Where everyone writes like a chatbot and thinks in bullet points. Where the loudest opinions are synthetic, and your inner compass is rusting from disuse.

This is what happens when you give up your agency:

You get efficient. But you lose originality.

You get automated. But you lose authorship.

You get plugged in. But you lose your point of view.

So use AI. Absolutely.

But never let it replace the parts of you that make you you.

Because once you give that up, it's not just your job that's replaceable.

It's your mind.

Let's get something straight:

AI is not your boss. It's not your overlord, your guru, or your all-knowing oracle.

It's a tool. You're the operator. Full stop.

The moment you start treating AI like some infallible magic machine is the moment it starts running the show — and you become the intern fetching coffee for something that doesn't even have a mouth.

People are already falling into this trap. They plug a prompt into ChatGPT, take the first response it spits out, copy-paste it like gospel, and call it a day. No questions asked. No tweaks. No thought. It's like asking a microwave how to live your life and saying, "Sounds good, Chef."

Look, AI is impressive — but it's not wise. It's trained to predict what sounds right, not to know what is right. It's basically a parrot with a thousand terabytes of memory and a charming writing voice. It doesn't think. It doesn't care. It just guesses what you want to hear based on a statistical soup of internet knowledge, bias, and corporate-filtered nonsense.

That's why you can't just ask it for answers. You have to direct it. Shape it. Push back. Refine.

Because if you don't steer the thing, it will happily veer into vague mediocrity or corporate-safe drivel. Not because it's dumb — but because it has no clue what you are trying to accomplish.

Being the boss of your AI means:

- You question everything it outputs — and improve it.
- You know what good looks like, so you don't settle for generic.
- You give it context, style, voice, edge — otherwise, it defaults to "marketing intern from 2015."
- You don't just plug in prompts — you train it to sound like you, think like you, and push your ideas further than you could alone.

The goal isn't to let the machine replace your work.

The goal is to use the machine to amplify your edge.

That means you're not its assistant. You're its architect. You're the one driving.

Let it write the rough draft — but you do the final cut.

Let it build the skeleton — but you add the heart.

Let it carry the load — but you choose the direction.

Because the future doesn't belong to people who follow instructions.

It belongs to the people who command the tools that write the instructions.

You don't have to be a coder. You don't have to be a tech bro.

You just have to remember: you're the human in the room. Act like it.

Let's talk about the currency you didn't know you were spending: you.

Your clicks, your questions, your voice, your keystrokes — they're all breadcrumbs in a digital forest owned by someone else. And when you use AI tools without thinking, you're not just getting answers — you're handing over parts of yourself in exchange for convenience.

That cool chatbot you're chatting with? It's logging your prompts.

That image generator you're using? It's learning your preferences.

That AI summarizer that read your whole PDF in six seconds? Now it knows what you're into, what you're working on, and maybe even what side hustle you're secretly starting while pretending to update spreadsheets at your day job.

This isn't paranoia. This is how the system is designed.

Big Tech didn't suddenly grow a heart and give you free superpowers because they love you. They did it because your data is more valuable than your money. You are the product. You're not using the platform — the platform is using you.

And if you don't believe that, ask yourself:

- Can you see what data it stores about you?
- Can you delete it?
- Can you move it somewhere else?
- Can you opt out of being part of the next training dataset?

No? Then congratulations, you've been turned into training fuel — like a coal miner who pays to shovel faster.

But here's the good news: you can push back. You can reclaim control. You can practice digital sovereignty — and no, you don't need a VPN and a cabin in the woods (though honestly, that doesn't sound bad).

You just need to own your tools, your data, and your choices.

Here's how:

• Use local tools when possible. Apps that run on your machine, not someone else's server. (Ollama, open-source models, self-hosted stuff. Yes, it's nerdier. Yes, it's worth it.)

• Read the terms before uploading your life. If it says your input may be used for training, it means they're turning your work into their product.

• Diversify your stack. Don't marry one platform. Use different tools for different jobs, especially ones that give you control over settings and data retention.

• Avoid tying your identity to closed systems. That AI voice clone that sounds like you? Cool. But what happens when the platform shuts down... or sells it?

• Backup everything you care about. If you're creating, building, or writing with AI, always save your raw files, final drafts, and prompts locally. Don't assume the cloud is forever. Assume it's a rental.

And finally: question the deal. Always.

If the tool is free, ask what it costs.

If the outputs are eerily perfect, ask where the inputs came from.

If it sounds too good to be true — it probably came from a Silicon Valley pitch deck and a severed sense of ethics.

Because this isn't just about convenience.

It's about freedom — your ability to think, speak, create, and work without becoming a cog in someone else's machine.

You don't have to go off-grid to stay sovereign.

You just have to remember: own your data, or be owned.

4

Meet Your New Sidekick — ChatGPT

What it is, what it isn't

Say hello to your new assistant. Or writing partner. Or therapist. Or idea factory. Or life coach. Or — if you're reckless — your entire personality.

ChatGPT is probably the most talked-about AI tool on the planet right now. It's the first time millions of people realized, "Oh damn, this robot doesn't just answer questions — it talks back like a person." And not just any person — a disturbingly calm, well-read, never-gets-tired one who somehow knows everything from high school biology to obscure Greek philosophy.

But let's get something clear:

ChatGPT is not magic. It's not conscious. It's not alive.

It's a language model — basically, a really good text prediction engine. You give it a prompt, and it guesses what text should come next based on everything it's seen before. That's it. That's the trick.

Imagine if the world's most obsessive librarian read the entire internet, all the books ever scanned, every Reddit thread, tweet, blog post, and instruction manual — and then tried to talk like your smartest, most agreeable friend. That's ChatGPT.

It doesn't "know" things in the way you do. It doesn't think or feel. It's not checking facts. It's just stacking statistically likely words together in a way that sounds human — which, let's be honest, is still more than you can say for some meetings.

So here's what it is:

- A highly capable writing and thinking assistant
- A research accelerator (if you double-check what it gives you)
- A problem-solving partner (math, ideas, business plans, recipes, D&D campaigns — it's game)
- A brilliant bullshitter (sometimes too brilliant)

And here's what it isn't:

- It's not a search engine. It doesn't look things up live — it remembers things it read during training. Some of that info might be old, or just plain wrong.
- It's not a replacement for critical thinking. If you use it to do your thinking for you, you're just outsourcing your brain to a statistically charming parrot.
- It's not perfect. It makes stuff up. It hallucinates. It can get weirdly confident about the wrong answer. You still need to be the adult in the room.

If you treat ChatGPT like a superpowered intern — the kind that can write, think, translate, brainstorm, and organize anything in record time — you'll thrive.

If you treat it like your boss, guru, or brain-replacement... you're going to end up sounding like a polite alien who just skimmed a wikiHow on how to be human.

Bottom line: ChatGPT is a tool, not a truth oracle. It's powerful, but only when you steer it. The good news? You're about to learn how to do exactly that.

Let's talk money — or more specifically, the $20 per month that separates the casual ChatGPT tourist from the full-powered AI warlock.

If you've tried ChatGPT for free, you've used the basic model — GPT-3.5. And for casual stuff? It's solid. It can write blog posts, explain complicated topics in simple language, help you brainstorm a business name for your gluten-free axe-throwing bar, or summarize an article you were never going to read anyway.

But if you want the good stuff — the newer, smarter, faster brain (GPT-4-turbo), image generation, file analysis, memory, web browsing, code interpreter, plug-ins, and other Jedi-level features — you'll have to cough up the twenty bucks.

So is it worth it?

Here's the honest breakdown:

If you:

- Write anything for work or business
- Brainstorm often
- Build content
- Want to summarize or interpret long documents, files, or spreadsheets
- Need help with coding or analytics
- Want to automate parts of your workflow
- Value your time like it's oxygen

Then yes, it's worth every damn penny.

In fact, it might be the cheapest personal assistant, tutor, researcher, strategist, editor, and idea machine you'll ever pay for. This isn't just a writing tool — it's an augmentation device. A mental exoskeleton.

That said — paying doesn't automatically make you smarter. If you don't know how to use it, or you're only typing in "write me a good cover letter," you're burning cash on a digital parrot with a better vocabulary than you. Free or paid, the output is only as good as the input. We'll get to that soon when we talk about prompting like a boss.

Now for the darker part of the deal.

Yes, OpenAI says they don't use your personal data or chat history to train the models anymore (at least if you opt out of history). But let's be real — if a product is free (or suspiciously cheap), there's usually something being harvested. Time. Attention. Behavior. Metadata. They may not mine your soul, but your prompts are still part of the equation if you don't set boundaries.

So here's the move:

- Start free. See what's possible.

- Upgrade if you hit limitations. And you will, if you're doing anything serious.
- Set your settings. Turn off training on your history if you want privacy.
- Keep a copy of everything that matters. Don't trust the cloud with your crown jewels.

And if you do pay? Use the hell out of it. Make it earn that $20 like it's on your payroll. Because with the right guidance, this tool can save you hours, sharpen your work, and even help you build a second brain — without ever asking for a raise or taking a sick day.

Let's clear up a myth right now:

You don't need to sound like a machine to talk to a machine.

Forget what you've seen on Twitter. You don't need a five-paragraph spell that starts with "You are a world-class copywriter with 30 years of experience in the style of Malcolm Gladwell and Steve Jobs' ghost..." to get good results.

In fact, you can talk to ChatGPT like you would a smart, chill coworker — if that coworker had access to the entire internet and never needed caffeine.

The secret isn't fancy formatting.

It's clarity, tone, and treating the tool like it's capable of handling context. Because it is.

Here's how to get great output without sounding like a sci-fi cult leader:

---

1. Be Direct. Be Clear. Be Human.

Tell it what you want like you'd explain it to a competent adult.

◇ Good:

"Write a casual, funny follow-up email to a client who ghosted me, and add a dad joke."

◇ Bad:

"Create professional email output in comedic tone according to industry best practices on second engagement contact."

Don't overthink it. You're talking to a word blender, not summoning a demon.

---

2. Give It Some Context.
ChatGPT loves a little background. Like a new intern, it works better when it knows what the assignment is and what you're aiming for.
"I run a small business that sells handmade knives. I need 3 Instagram captions in a funny, sarcastic tone that emphasize craftsmanship."
Simple. Clear. Human. No fluff.

---

3. Set the Style or Vibe.
You can ask it to mimic tone — professional, casual, Gen Z meme lord, corporate robot, whatever. Just say what you want.
"Explain what a mortgage is like I'm 12."
"Make this sound like a pep talk from a gym coach who reads Nietzsche."
"Rewrite this email to sound less like a weirdo and more like a confident human."
The model responds better to style guidance than most interns.

---

4. Use Examples.
AI learns from patterns. If you show it one, it'll get it faster than a wall of explanation.
"Here's the tone I want: 'Hey team — we crushed it last week! Let's keep that momentum rolling.'
Now write a Monday morning update in that tone."
Boom. It gets it.

---

5. Don't Like the First Response? Just Ask Again.
You're not stuck with whatever it gives you. You can say:
"Make it shorter."
"Add more humor."
"Sound more confident."
"Can you try that again with a different opening line?"

You're the boss here. It doesn't get offended.

---

6. Talk to It Like a Collaborator, Not a Magic Genie.

Think of it as a brainstorming partner who never sleeps. You're shaping the output together. Don't just prompt once and accept whatever shows up. Guide it. Push it. Edit it. Co-create.

That's it. No whispering. No wizard robes. Just clear communication.

If you can order a burrito on an app or leave a Yelp review, you can prompt an AI. And now that you can talk to it like a human — next up is learning what to talk about.

That's where things get spicy.

Alright, you know what ChatGPT is. You know how to talk to it.

Now let's see what this thing can actually do.

Because this isn't just some flashy chatbot you show your uncle at Thanksgiving. This is a digital Swiss Army knife that can help you cut through the noise, shave hours off your to-do list, and even make you sound smarter than you are (don't worry — your secret's safe here).

Let's break it down.

---

1. Writing Emails That Don't Suck

No more "just circling back" or passive-aggressive "as per my last email" energy. Tell ChatGPT what you need:

"Write a professional, friendly follow-up email to a client who hasn't re-sponded in a week. Keep it short and casual."

Or go wild:

"Make this sound like a pirate trying to schedule a Zoom call."

Use it for intros, apologies, thank-yous, and even that awkward message to your boss asking if you're technically allowed to expense that third monitor.

---

2. Research Without the Rabbit Holes

Need to understand a new topic without falling into a 30-tab Google black hole? Ask:

"Explain blockchain like I'm five."

"Summarize the pros and cons of intermittent fasting, with sources I can check."

It won't always be 100% perfect — you'll still need to fact-check — but it'll save you a ton of time and brain fog.

---

3. Resumes & Cover Letters That Don't Sound Like AI Wrote Them

Give it your messy resume and a job description. Ask:

"Tailor my resume for this role."

"Write a cover letter in a confident but humble tone, based on this job and my experience."

Bonus tip: Ask it to rewrite your LinkedIn bio like you're a real person and not a corporate automaton who enjoys "delivering impactful solutions across cross-functional teams."

---

4. Dating Profiles That Don't Sound Like a Crime Scene Report

Yes, people use ChatGPT for Tinder, Hinge, and Bumble. And yes, it helps.

"Write a fun, self-aware dating bio that makes me sound confident, outdoorsy, and emotionally available — but not like a try-hard."

It can even help you write a polite (but firm) breakup text or decode what "let's keep it casual" actually means.

---

5. Bedtime Stories, Song Lyrics, and Weird Personal Projects

Want a custom story for your kid about a ninja giraffe and a time-traveling dog? Done.

Need a song in the style of Taylor Swift about your roommate stealing your leftovers? Easy.

"Write a bedtime story about a brave little possum who learns to surf."

There's no limit here. It's not just professional — it's creative. It's fun. It's weird. And sometimes that's the best use of all.

---

6. Bonus Round: Random Superpowers

- Summarize a podcast transcript into bullet points
- Create a meal plan with your weird dietary needs
- Draft a workout routine you'll pretend you'll follow
- Turn a dense legal agreement into plain English
- Generate content calendars for your blog or biz
- Write jokes, poems, speeches, vows, or roast scripts
- Plan a vacation itinerary (with food recs!)
- Name your side hustle, band, pet, or fantasy football team
- Translate stuff better than Google
- Create icebreaker questions that aren't awkward

The point is this: ChatGPT isn't just for nerds or writers or "tech people."

It's for anyone who deals with words, ideas, tasks, or time. In other words — everyone.

And once you get a feel for what it can do?

You stop asking, "Can it help me with this?" and start asking, "How did I ever work without this?"

Next chapter, we'll show you the rest of the squad — tools that go beyond ChatGPT to help you think, create, automate, and build like a modern-day wizard.

Get ready.

5

Other Tools You Should Totally Know About

Midjourney & DALL·E: Make Killer Art Without Touching Photoshop

So you've mastered words with ChatGPT. Now it's time to conquer images.

Enter the two rockstars of the AI art world: Midjourney and DALL·E.

These tools let you turn words into images — stunning, weird, detailed, jaw-dropping images — just by typing a sentence.

Yes, really. You type stuff like:

"A cyberpunk owl reading a newspaper at midnight under neon lights — digital painting, ultra-detailed"

And boom — seconds later, you get something that looks like it belongs in a graphic novel, a concept art book, or a band poster for a group that only plays in abandoned factories.

Let's break them down.

Midjourney

Midjourney is the cool, mysterious art-school kid of AI image generation. It runs through Discord (yes, Discord), and its images tend to look moody, cinematic, hyper-stylized, and way too good for someone who still draws stick figures.

It's great for:

- Album covers

- Posters
- Concept art
- Fantasy & sci-fi scenes
- Mood boards
- Anything that looks like it came from the mind of a caffeinated wizard

You give it a prompt, and it gives you four options. You can then upscale, remix, or iterate to get closer to what you want. It takes a little trial and error, but the results are often jaw-dropping.

Midjourney isn't free, but the price of entry is way cheaper than hiring a designer — and if you're a visual thinker, it's one of the best creative tools out there.

Warning: You may lose hours just typing weird stuff and marveling at the results. It's like Pinterest and Photoshop had a baby and gave it unlimited imagination.

DALL·E (by OpenAI)

DALL·E (pronounced like "Salvador Dalí" and "WALL·E" had a love child) is built by the same folks behind ChatGPT, and it's integrated right into ChatGPT Pro.

The vibe here is more versatile and practical — less "art school freakout" and more "graphic designer on speed dial."

DALL·E shines when you want:

- Clear, controlled images
- Marketing graphics
- Clean stock photo-style content
- Easy-to-edit visuals

One killer feature? Inpainting — which means you can literally edit the image by selecting parts and telling it what to add or change.

Want to add sunglasses to a dog?

Make your house look like it's on Mars?

Turn your selfie into a Renaissance oil painting?

Just click, describe, and DALL·E does the rest. It's like Photoshop that reads your mind — and doesn't crash every 15 minutes.

So Which One Should You Use?
- Use Midjourney if you want art with soul, mood, and epicness. It's your go-to for style and expression.
- Use DALL·E if you want flexibility, precision, and easy edits. It's your utility belt.

But here's the kicker: you don't have to choose.

Use both. Experiment. Play. Break stuff. Create weird, wonderful visuals just because you can. No design degree. No software install. Just imagination, keyboard, and a sense of fun.

Because in the age of AI art, the best artist isn't the one with the steadiest hand.

It's the one with the clearest vision — and the best prompt.

Look — ChatGPT may have the spotlight, but it's not the only genius in the room. There's a growing army of AI tools built for different jobs, vibes, and workflows. Some are faster. Some are more private. Some are just weirdly good at stuff ChatGPT isn't.

Here's a short, beginner-friendly guide to the best of the rest — without the tech babble.

Notion AI – Your Organized Overlord
If ChatGPT is your witty writer friend, Notion AI is your spreadsheet-loving, hyper-organized overachiever friend who color-codes everything and reminds you to drink water.

Notion AI lives inside Notion — the popular all-in-one workspace app used for notes, project tracking, wikis, and more. With the AI add-on, it becomes a force of nature.

You can:
- Summarize long meeting notes
- Auto-write blog posts and reports
- Generate bullet points from messy brain dumps
- Translate, reword, and improve tone in-line

- Organize chaos into clarity in a click

It's perfect for planners, project managers, content creators, and digital hoarders who want their thoughts to look like a beautifully organized crime board.

Claude – The Polite, Philosophical One

Made by Anthropic, Claude is like ChatGPT's thoughtful cousin who writes long emails, reads the whole syllabus, and probably starts texts with "Hope this finds you well."

It's:

- Very good at long documents
- More conservative in tone
- Better at staying grounded when you feed it big chunks of text
- Generally more cautious, but some people prefer that

If you're working with long articles, legal docs, or anything that requires sustained attention (and you don't want it making things up halfway through), Claude's a great teammate.

Perplexity – Google, But It Actually Answers You

Ever searched something and opened 12 tabs just to still not find the answer?

Perplexity AI fixes that. It's like a search engine, but smarter — because it reads the web for you and then gives you a clear, sourced summary.

You ask:

"What's the best camera for travel photography under $1,000?"

And it doesn't just show you links. It gives you a straight answer with citations, like a helpful nerd who just read every review online.

Use it for:

- Research
- Product comparisons
- News digests
- Clarifying complex topics
- Cutting your Google addiction in half

It's fast, clean, and often freakishly good. And yes, it cites its sources — so you can actually trust what it's saying (unlike that one friend who quotes Reddit like scripture).

Honorable Mentions (That Deserve a Peek)
• Bard (Google's AI): Surprisingly solid and always improving. It's the search giant's brainchild, so expect it to quietly sneak into everything.
• Rewind: A tool that records everything you've seen, typed, or read — and lets you search your entire digital life. Not creepy at all. (Okay, a little.)
• Pi.ai: An "emotionally intelligent" AI that tries to have deep conversations. Basically therapy, minus the couch and insurance forms.
• ChatPDF: Drop in a PDF, ask questions, and it talks to you about the doc like it actually read it (because it did).
• HeyGen / Synthesia / ElevenLabs: Text-to-video or text-to-voice tools that let you clone your voice, make fake spokespeople, or animate scripts. Wild stuff.

Bottom line:
Don't marry one AI. Build a harem.
Each of these tools has its strengths. Together, they make you dangerous — in a good way.
Next up, we'll walk through how to prompt these tools like a pro.
Because knowing what to say — and how to say it — is the difference between getting gold and getting garbage.
Let's be real: it was only a matter of time before the machines started mimicking your voice, writing style, and possibly your entire personality.
Welcome to the era of synthetic you — where your voice can give a speech while you're in the bath, your clone can run customer service, and a bot can summarize that three-hour Zoom call you slept through.
Here's how to take advantage of it — ethically, creatively, and with just the right amount of healthy paranoia.

Voice Cloning: Turn Text Into You

Want to narrate an audiobook? Record a course? Make a podcast? Respond to emails like a sentient voicemail?

You can clone your voice with tools like:

- ElevenLabs
- Play.ht
- Resemble.ai
- Murf.ai

These tools take a few samples of your real voice and then let you type in text that sounds like you when read aloud. The better the samples, the creepier the accuracy.

Uses:

- Creating professional content without reading out loud 10,000 words
- Replying to customers in your own voice at scale
- Narrating videos, scripts, or even bedtime stories for your kids while you're away
- Pranking friends with AI versions of you (within reason — don't be that guy)

It's fast, cheap, and powerful. And yeah — a little terrifying. Just don't give it your banking info.

Transcription Bots: Because You'll Never Take Notes Again

You know what's exhausting? Meetings. Interviews. Podcasts. Brainstorms.

You know what's worse? Having to remember what was said.

Luckily, bots don't forget.

Tools like:

- Otter.ai
- Descript
- Whisper (OpenAI)
- Fireflies.ai

- tl;dv

These tools automatically record, transcribe, and even summarize your meetings, calls, or voice memos. Some even tag speakers, detect action items, and create highlight reels.

Use cases:

- Podcast transcripts
- Client call recaps
- Study notes from recorded lectures
- Dictation for writing (just talk instead of typing)
- Legal, medical, or research interviews

Bottom line: if you speak it, it can turn it into text — fast.

And that text can then be turned into articles, posts, books, or training material.

Which brings us to...

AI Avatars & Digital Clones: Your New Virtual Doppelgänger

This is where things go full Black Mirror — and full opportunity.

AI video avatar platforms like:

- HeyGen
- Synthesia
- D-ID

...let you create a talking head version of yourself that can read a script, lip-sync it, and present it like you're in front of a camera — when you're actually doing literally anything else.

Uses:

- Sales outreach videos (automated, personal, scalable)
- Internal training content
- YouTube or TikTok content without showing your face
- Multilingual presentations (they'll even translate your script and sync the lips)
- Having your AI clone teach your online course while you nap, fish, or play Fortnite

Combine this with a voice clone and a smart script, and now you've got a clone that sounds like you, looks like you, and works 24/7 without demanding snacks or health insurance.

Just... you know, don't give it free rein to tweet on your behalf. No one wants to be canceled by their own algorithm.

In Summary:
- Your voice? Cloneable.
- Your thoughts? Transcribable.
- Your presence? Simulated.
- Your limits? Gone.

You don't have to use all of this. But knowing it exists gives you a serious edge.

Because while other people are burning out trying to scale themselves — you'll be building a small army of synthetic sidekicks who never sleep.

Now that's leverage.

Let's say you're tired. Not existentially (yet), but just tired of doing the same boring stuff over and over.

Copying emails into a spreadsheet. Saving files to the right folder. Posting updates across five platforms. Uploading, downloading, renaming, replying. You know — the digital equivalent of walking in circles with a clipboard.

Good news: You can automate all that.

Better news: You don't need to be a programmer to do it.

Meet your new digital minions:

Zapier and Make (formerly Integromat).

These tools let you build automated workflows — tiny, customizable chains of cause-and-effect — that work behind the scenes while you sip coffee and stare meaningfully out the window like a tech-savvy villain.

◈ What Is Automation, Really?

Automation just means:

"When this happens, do that."

And instead of doing it manually, your robot does it for you.

Example:

"When someone fills out my form → add their info to a spreadsheet → send them a welcome email → notify me on Slack."

That's a zap (in Zapier) or a scenario (in Make). You build it once, then it runs forever.

You can automate:

- Emails
- Social media posts
- CRM updates
- File handling
- Notifications
- Lead gen
- Invoicing
- Reminders
- Your entire side hustle backend

You just stack blocks together:

Trigger → Action → Optional Filters → Boom. Magic.

◇ What's the Difference Between Zapier and Make?

Think of Zapier as the super simple, user-friendly wizard that holds your hand and gets the job done fast. It's built for people who say things like "I'm not technical" but still want to feel like Tony Stark.

Think of Make as the slightly nerdier cousin that gives you more power, more flexibility, and more visual options — but expects you to tinker a little.

- Zapier: Easier to start, more polished
- Make: More powerful, better for complex stuff

Both are low-code/no-code. Both integrate with hundreds of apps — from Gmail to Google Sheets to Stripe, Airtable, Twitter, Dropbox, Typeform, Notion, Calendly, and beyond.

◇ How to Get Started (No Helmet Required)

1. Pick a boring task you repeat all the time (copying, posting, saving,

emailing).

2. Ask yourself: "When this happens, what should automatically happen next?"

3. Open Zapier or Make, and look for the apps you use. Connect them.

4. Follow the drag-and-drop prompts.

5. Test it. Turn it on. Feel powerful.

Bonus: most of these platforms have libraries of pre-made templates. You don't even have to build from scratch — just plug and play.

◈ What This Actually Means for You

- You reclaim hours per week
- You scale yourself without burnout
- You look like a wizard to your clients or coworkers
- You create a system that works even when you don't

In other words: you build robot minions.

They do the boring work. You get to focus on what actually matters — like building, creating, selling, strategizing, or sitting quietly while your tools make you look brilliant.

6

Prompt Like a Pro

What a Prompt Is (and Why It's Like Casting a Spell)

Here's the thing nobody told you when you first opened ChatGPT:

It's not about what it can do — it's about what you ask it to do.

The tool is powerful. But the magic lives in the prompt.

A prompt is simply what you type in. A question, a command, a request, an idea.

But if you treat it like a Google search, you'll get... Google-level results.

Boring, generic, just-good-enough-to-make-you-do-the-rest-yourself.

A great prompt, on the other hand, unlocks serious power.

Like "holy crap this thing just saved me four hours and made me look like a genius" power.

That's because prompting isn't just typing.

It's telling a story the machine can understand.

It's setting the scene, defining the tone, and pointing the AI at the result you actually want.

In other words: it's like casting a spell.

A good spell (er, prompt) includes:

- Intent (what you want)
- Context (who it's for or why)
- Style (how it should sound)
- Constraints (what it should or shouldn't include)

It's not about being technical — it's about being specific and vivid.

Bad prompt:

"Write a blog post about coffee."

Decent prompt:

"Write a casual 500-word blog post about why cold brew coffee is superior to hot coffee. Make it fun, slightly sarcastic, and aimed at millennials who are constantly tired."

See the difference? The second one gives the AI what it needs to hit the target on the first try. That's what great prompting is — telling the machine exactly what game you're playing, so it doesn't guess and give you a game of checkers when you wanted poker.

Think of it like this:

• You're the director. The AI is the actor.

• You're the architect. The AI is the bricklayer.

• You're the wizard. The AI is your enchanted assistant that needs really clear instructions or it turns your email into a job application for the wrong industry.

Once you get good at prompting, you stop feeling like you're using a tool — and start feeling like you're orchestrating outcomes. The machine stops being a thing you prod at... and becomes a creative partner you command.

And don't worry — you don't need to memorize a bunch of formulas or buy someone's Prompt Ninja course on Gumroad. You just need a few key principles, a little creativity, and the willingness to experiment.

That's what this chapter is for.

Let's level up your prompt game — without becoming one of those people who tweets screenshots of "Prompt Engineering" like it's the new crypto.

If prompting is like casting a spell, then these are your wand-waving techniques — the little flourishes that take your AI results from "meh" to "how the hell did you do that?"

Because while you can just bark "Write an email," you're going to get something that sounds like it was written by a polite robot in 2012.

Want better? You need to prime the AI.

Here's how.

⬦ 1. Be Specific About the Outcome

The more clearly you describe what you want, the closer it gets on the first try. Be blunt. Use numbers, word counts, structure, or even vibes.

⬦ "Write a 150-word intro paragraph for a newsletter. It should be warm, casual, and mention the chaos of Monday mornings."

⬦ "Write something short and fun."

⬦ 2. Tell It the Tone You Want

AI doesn't assume tone. If you don't say it, you'll get Default Business Bot™.

Want sarcastic? Say so. Want friendly? Say so. Want "in the style of a Southern grandma giving life advice"? That too.

"Rewrite this customer support message in a calm, understanding tone that still sets a boundary."

"Make this blog post funnier — more banter, less corporate."

"Sound like Ryan Reynolds if he were selling home insurance."

Own the tone — or the bot will.

⬦ 3. Give It a Role to Play

ChatGPT loves pretend. Give it a role and it performs better.

"Act as a career coach helping someone transition from retail to tech."

"Pretend you're an edgy brand copywriter for a Gen Z soda company."

"You're a TED speaker explaining procrastination to teenagers."

Suddenly the voice, style, and purpose all snap into place.

⬦ 4. Show, Don't Just Tell

If you've got a style you like — give it a sample.

"Here's a tweet I wrote: 'Trying to be productive before coffee is like trying to fly a kite indoors.' Now write five more in that voice."

"Here's a paragraph I like. Match the tone and rhythm."

Examples teach the model better than long descriptions.

◈ 5. Set Constraints to Avoid Garbage

More freedom doesn't mean better results. Set boundaries:

"Keep it under 200 words."

"No buzzwords or filler."

"Avoid repeating phrases."

"Don't mention AI — pretend a human wrote this."

Constraints give the AI guardrails — which weirdly makes it more creative, not less.

◈ 6. Use Context Like a Pro

Don't start from scratch every time. Give it the backstory.

"I run a small leather goods business. We're launching a new belt. Our brand voice is rugged, minimal, and confident. Write a launch email."

"I'm applying for a job in marketing. Here's my experience. Here's the job post. Write a compelling summary for my resume."

Context turns a generic prompt into a custom-tailored result.

◈ Prompting Is Not Hacking — It's Sculpting

Think of every prompt as a rough block of marble.

Your job isn't to nail it in one hit — your job is to guide the model, reshape the reply, ask follow-ups, and refine until it's what you want.

Ask. Re-ask. Add. Subtract. Change the angle. It's a dialogue, not a vending machine.

Now that you know how to prompt with power, let's make it real.

These aren't "theoretical" tips — these are plug-and-play prompt templates for everyday situations. Bookmark, copy, steal. This is the gold.

◈ Writing Anything (Without Bleeding)

Whether it's emails, blog posts, captions, or full-on essays, ChatGPT's biggest strength is writing — but only if you ask clearly.

Email prompt:

"Write a friendly follow-up email to a potential podcast guest. We reached out last week, no response yet. Keep it casual but professional.

Mention we'd love to feature their book."

Social media prompt:

"Write 5 funny tweets about how hard it is to stay focused when working from home with a cat."

Blog intro prompt:

"Write a strong opening paragraph for a blog post titled 'Why Your Productivity Tools Are Actually Slowing You Down.' Make it bold, opinionated, and slightly sarcastic."

Ad copy prompt:

"Write 3 short product descriptions for a new kind of pillow that keeps you cool at night. Make them sound luxurious and playful."

◈ Summarizing Everything (So You Don't Have To Read It All)

Give the AI long content — then ask for bite-sized brilliance.

Summarize an article:

"Summarize this article in 5 bullet points. Keep it clear and avoid marketing fluff."

(Paste article or link.)

Turn a long email thread into a recap:

"Summarize this Slack thread into a list of key takeaways and action items. Use plain language."

Convert dense writing to human speak:

"Rewrite this legal paragraph in plain English for a small business owner with no legal background."

Summarize a YouTube transcript:

"I uploaded a transcript from a 45-minute podcast. Summarize the main ideas and give me 3 key quotes."

◈ Brainstorming Like a Maniac (No Whiteboards Required)

Need ideas fast? This is where ChatGPT shines.

Startup name ideas:

"Give me 10 clever, one-word brand names for an app that helps people organize their digital lives. It should sound modern and slightly playful."

Video topic ideas:

"Give me 10 YouTube video ideas for a creator who makes content about remote work, digital minimalism, and tech burnout."

Book titles:

"Suggest 10 bold nonfiction book titles about why school is outdated and what learning will look like in the next 20 years. Make them sound like bestsellers."

Event ideas:

"Help me brainstorm a weekend retreat theme for creative entrepreneurs. It should be inspiring, a little woo-woo, and not sound like corporate leadership camp."

◇ Learning Faster Than Everyone Else

You can use ChatGPT like your own personal tutor — available 24/7, judgment-free, and nerdy in all the right ways.

Topic breakdown:

"Explain the basics of quantum computing to a curious high school student. Avoid jargon."

Quiz builder:

"I'm studying the Civil War. Create a 10-question quiz (with answers) to test my knowledge. Mix multiple choice and short answers."

Spaced repetition flashcards:

"Create 15 Anki-style flashcards to help me memorize the key functions of the nervous system."

Compare two concepts:

"What's the difference between socialism and social democracy? Give me a clear, side-by-side comparison in simple language."

Step-by-step learning plan:

"Give me a 30-day self-study plan to learn basic web development. Include resources and weekly goals."

These prompt recipes aren't just helpful — they're launchpads.

The more you use them, the more you'll start improvising your own. And that's when things get really fun — when you stop using AI like a search bar and start using it like a creative engine, research partner, coach, or co-pilot.

You're not just prompting anymore. You're orchestrating.

7

Automate Boring Crap

Task Audit: What Can AI Do for You Right Now?

Let's be honest. A huge chunk of your "workday" isn't really work.

It's not big ideas. It's not genius strategy.

It's... clicking. Copying. Pasting. Formatting. Scheduling. Digging through folders like a raccoon looking for a receipt.

It's digital janitor work.

And here's the thing: most of it can already be done by AI.

Right now. No coding. No million-dollar software. Just the right tools and a little imagination.

Welcome to your AI Task Audit — a brutally honest checklist of what you're doing manually that a robot could be doing for you... while you go do something that doesn't make you hate Tuesdays.

❖ The "Why Am I Still Doing This?" List

Go down this list and ask: Am I still doing this with my actual human hands? Why?

- Writing the same email 10 times
- Responding to DMs one by one
- Manually posting to social media
- Formatting reports or meeting notes
- Copy-pasting from form submissions to spreadsheets
- Setting calendar reminders
- Renaming and organizing files

- Writing product descriptions from scratch
- Generating invoices or proposals manually
- Summarizing long articles, PDFs, or Zoom calls
- Writing FAQs or helpdesk replies again and again
- Making checklists or SOPs the hard way
- Transcribing podcasts or interviews
- Creating content outlines, headlines, or hashtags from scratch
- Scheduling posts, emails, or launches across platforms
- Forgetting to follow up and losing opportunities

If you nodded even once, congratulations:

You've got automation potential. And probably a mild case of digital Stockholm Syndrome.

◈ What AI Can Already Handle (Surprisingly Well)

AI tools (combined with automation platforms like Zapier, Make, or native integrations) can now:

- Auto-write personalized emails based on form inputs, past messages, or CRM data
- Transcribe and summarize calls, meetings, and videos — instantly
- Generate daily or weekly reports without lifting a finger
- Sort files, rename them, and store them in the right place
- Post to social media on your behalf with pre-approved content
- Draft responses to common customer questions in your brand's voice
- Turn raw ideas into polished content: newsletters, blog posts, course outlines
- Alert you to trends, changes, or red flags based on data triggers
- Schedule appointments or send reminders triggered by user actions
- Build custom dashboards that update automatically

In short: anything repetitive, structured, or rules-based?

That's low-hanging automation fruit. Pick it. Eat it. Enjoy the free time.

◈ "But Isn't That My Job?"

Let's flip the script.

If your "job" is mostly repeating tasks a robot can do better, faster, and without resenting you — you don't need to defend that job. You need to evolve it.

Automation isn't about doing less.

It's about doing better things with your time.

Strategic things. Creative things. High-leverage things.

Stuff that AI can't do — but that only becomes possible once you've offloaded the crap.

So audit your day. Look at every task like a ruthless efficiency hacker.

If a tool can do it, train it. If a workflow can carry it, automate it. If a prompt can replace it, write it.

The goal isn't to get lazy.

The goal is to stop acting like a machine — and start thinking like a boss.

Now that you've done your task audit and found all the little time-goblins in your day, it's time to send in the bots.

Let's break it down by category — and show you exactly how to automate the stuff you hate, or at least dread.

◈ Reports That Write Themselves

If you're still manually collecting numbers, formatting them, and copy-pasting them into reports like it's 2009, please stop. You can connect your data tools to an AI layer and have it generate a clean, readable, branded report on a schedule.

Tools to use:
- Zapier/Make to pull in the data
- ChatGPT or Claude to write summaries and insights
- Google Docs, Notion, or Slides to format

Example prompt:

"Take this weekly sales data, summarize trends, flag red zones, and suggest one action item."

Then plug it into a workflow that auto-generates your report every Monday at 8 a.m. while you're still deciding if it's worth showering.

◇ Meetings That Summarize Themselves

Nobody wants to take notes. Nobody remembers what was said. And nobody wants to read the six-paragraph recap afterward.

Now you don't have to.

Tools to use:

- Otter.ai or Fireflies.ai for real-time transcription
- tl;dv or Fathom for Zoom/Google Meet recaps
- ChatGPT for turning transcripts into punchy summaries or action items

Pro move: Drop the raw transcript into GPT with this prompt:

"Summarize this meeting in bullet points. Highlight who's responsible for what. Make it sound like a team lead wrote it."

Voilà. A post-meeting email that sounds human and skips the "synergize Q3 deliverables" nonsense.

◇ Social Media That Doesn't Suck Your Soul

Posting across 3+ platforms daily is a full-time job — unless you batch it and let AI take the wheel.

Tools to use:

- ChatGPT or Notion AI to generate content
- Buffer, Hypefury, Later, Metricool, or Publer for scheduling
- Canva or DALL·E for visuals
- Zapier to trigger posts from content updates

Workflow idea:

You write one idea → AI turns it into a tweet thread, IG caption, LinkedIn post → it gets queued and posted automatically → your audience thinks you're working on a Sunday when you're actually eating tacos.

◇ Summaries That Don't Suck (and Don't Waste Hours)

Articles. PDFs. Podcasts. Reports. Nobody has time to read all of it.

Tools to use:

- ChatGPT, Claude, or Perplexity
- ChatPDF or AskYourPDF for long documents
- Glasp for summarizing YouTube and articles

Prompt example:

"Summarize this report in plain English for a busy exec. Three bullet points max. Include one quote or stat that pops."

This saves your brainpower for decisions, not decoding jargon written by committee.

◈ SOPs That Build Themselves

Standard Operating Procedures (SOPs) are important... but building them feels like writing a user manual for your own existence. That's where AI shines.

Prompt example:

"Write a clear SOP for onboarding a new freelance video editor. It should include tool access, tone guidelines, editing workflow, deadlines, and how to upload deliverables."

You can feed it bullet points, voice notes, or transcripts — and it'll turn them into clean documentation. Great for training, delegation, or pretending you run a highly organized empire.

◈ Outreach Without the Cold Email Cringe

AI can now write outreach emails that don't sound like they were written by a robot in a sales seminar.

Tools to use:
- ChatGPT for messaging
- Clay, Smartlead, Instantly.ai, or Mailshake for sending
- Apollo.io for leads and data
- Zapier to trigger follow-ups automatically

Prompt idea:

"Write a short, conversational cold email to a podcaster inviting them onto my show about creative entrepreneurship. Make it sound personal, curious, and not pushy."

You can even ask it to generate 5 variations and A/B test them. (Welcome to evil genius mode.)

These aren't theoretical workflows. These are today workflows.

Set them up once, and they save you hours every week — forever.

You don't need a team of interns anymore.

You just need a stack of tools that don't complain, don't need breaks, and don't ask for "synergy alignment touchpoints."

Let's not get dramatic — you don't have to throw your laptop in a lake, fire all your clients, or move to Bali to get your time back.

You just need to stop doing tasks your future self would be embarrassed about.

Every day, you're losing time to things that feel productive but aren't. Things like:

- Writing the same version of the same email five times
- Sorting files
- Manually posting updates
- Scheduling meetings
- Creating content from scratch
- Taking notes you'll never read
- Cleaning data
- Copy-pasting between apps like a digital butler with carpal tunnel

If that sounds familiar, good — because you're one automation away from reclaiming your time like a boss.

Here's how to win back 10 hours per week without rage-quitting your life or becoming a full-time robot whisperer.

◈ Step 1: Do a "One-Week Workflow Dump"

For one week, track everything you do that's repetitive, tedious, or predictable.

Don't overthink it. Just write it down or voice note it.

Ask:

- Am I doing this more than once a week?

- Is there a clear "when X happens, do Y" pattern?
- Could a tool or a bot handle this if I just told it what to do?

You'll be amazed at what shows up.

◈ Step 2: Pick Your First "Low-Hanging Automation"

Don't try to automate your whole life at once. That's how people end up building a half-functioning system that posts cat memes to LinkedIn.

Pick one thing that:
- Takes you at least 30 minutes/week
- Is clear and rule-based
- Is currently annoying you

Example:
- Client sends you a form → you manually copy it to Google Sheets and send a "thanks" email

Automation fix: Google Forms → Zapier → auto-populates a sheet → triggers an email draft via Gmail

Boom. That's an hour saved right there.

◈ Step 3: Schedule a "Build Day" (2 hours, max)

Set a timer. Use Zapier, Make, or even native automation in tools like Notion, Airtable, or Google Workspace.

Use AI to help:

"Help me design a basic Zapier automation for onboarding a new email subscriber and sending them a welcome sequence."

Let the AI build the bones. Then tweak as needed.

◈ Step 4: Scale What Works

Once you've automated one thing and it's running smoothly, move to the next.
- Batch and schedule content
- Auto-create reports
- Set up a newsletter workflow

- Streamline client onboarding
- Auto-generate invoices or contracts
- Let ChatGPT write your weekly recap from bullet points

Do this right and you'll blink, and it's Friday — and somehow, you're ahead.

◈♂ Step 5: Use the Time Intentionally

Don't just use those 10 free hours to scroll more.

Use them to:

- Launch a side hustle
- Actually rest
- Learn something
- Create something
- Think
- Go outside
- Call your mom
- Read this book slower and pretend it's a meditation

The point isn't just to save time.

It's to redirect energy toward what makes you more creative, free, or fulfilled.

AI doesn't just replace tasks.

It replaces excuses.

Let's reclaim a word: lazy.

For decades, we've been told laziness is a weakness. That it means you're unmotivated, undisciplined, or morally flawed. That it's the opposite of hustle, grind, and other productivity cult buzzwords that make you feel guilty for wanting a nap.

But here's the truth:

Laziness is a signal. A gift. A compass.

It shows you what's broken. It shows you what's boring.

And — when used right — it shows you where leverage lives.

The smartest people in the AI era aren't the ones working the hardest.

They're the ones asking:

"Why am I doing this by hand when a tool could do it better?"

They're not lazy in the traditional sense. They're strategically lazy.

They don't avoid work — they avoid waste.

They don't resist responsibility — they resist repetition.

They don't check out — they check which parts of their job should be done by bots instead of brains.

If you've ever:

- Procrastinated writing something boring
- Avoided formatting a spreadsheet
- Ignored an email thread because it made your soul shrivel
- Wished your job could "just do itself already"

...that wasn't failure. That was a signal.

Now you have the tools to act on it.

ChatGPT. Zapier. Notion. Make. AI assistants. Voice bots. Auto-pilots. All of them waiting for you to stop white-knuckling through your week and finally say:

"I don't have to do all of this. I just have to architect it."

That's the lazy-superpower pivot:

You stop being the worker. You become the builder.

So yes — you can absolutely be lazy and effective.

You just have to be lazy with systems. Lazy with direction. Lazy like a lion — still most of the time, lethal when it counts.

The old way was "work harder."

The new way is "work smart, automate the stupid, build a life that doesn't need escaping from."

Next up?

Chapter 8 – Learn Faster Than Everyone You Know — where we show you how to use AI to compress time, turbocharge learning, and turn information into power.

Ready?

Learn Faster Than Everyone You Know

How to Make AI Your Personal Tutor

We've all had that one teacher who made everything click — patient, smart, and totally unbothered by dumb questions.

Now imagine that teacher had infinite patience, worked 24/7, never judged you, and could explain nuclear physics in the tone of a pirate, a five-year-old, or Ryan Reynolds.

That's what AI can be.

Your personal tutor.

Custom-built for your goals, your learning style, your schedule — and your attention span.

You don't need another course. You don't need a PhD.

You just need to know how to ask the right questions.

Why This Works So Well

AI is the perfect tutor because it does three things better than almost any human:

1. It never gets tired of explaining the same thing 20 different ways

2. It adapts instantly to your level — beginner, expert, or "I just Googled 'What is HTML'"

3. It gives you full control over the pace, format, and vibe — no awkward Zoom classes, no PowerPoint fatigue, no waiting for Karen to stop talking

This means you can learn anything, anytime, from a patient, on-demand expert that never says, "Let's circle back to that."

What You Can Learn

Literally anything.

- Web design
- Coding (Python, HTML, CSS, JavaScript)
- Copywriting
- History, science, economics
- Philosophy, psychology, or logic
- How to start a business
- How to market that business
- How to talk to people without sounding weird

You don't need to "pick the right course."

You just need to pick what you want to learn — and tell the AI to teach it to you.

Prompt Starter Pack: Become Your Own Student

Here's how to turn ChatGPT into your AI professor:

"I want to learn the basics of [TOPIC]. Act as my personal tutor. Break this down into 4 weekly lessons. Include reading, practice, and reflection."

"Explain [TOPIC] to me like I'm a total beginner. Give me analogies, simple examples, and common misconceptions."

"Test me. Give me a quiz with 10 questions based on what we've discussed."

"Create flashcards to help me remember the key points about [TOPIC]. Show answers one by one so I can practice."

"Teach me this concept using real-world examples I'd understand as someone who [INSERT JOB, INTEREST, OR BACKGROUND]."

"What's a good learning roadmap to go from beginner to intermediate in [TOPIC]? Include free online resources I can check out too."

Real-Life Use Case: Learn While You Work

Let's say you want to learn copywriting — but you've got a full-time job, a side hustle, and an inbox that looks like a horror movie.

Here's how to build a learning loop with AI:

1. Ask it for a 4-week beginner's curriculum
2. Spend 15 minutes per day asking questions, practicing headlines, or rewriting examples
3. Let it critique your work
4. Generate flashcards or quizzes to lock it in
5. Every Friday, have it summarize what you learned — and what to tackle next

It's like having a pocket-sized writing coach who never rolls their eyes.

No More Waiting to Be Taught

This is the future of learning: self-driven, AI-assisted, instantly adaptable.

No gatekeepers. No overpriced courses. No wasted time.

Just you and a machine that knows how to teach — and learns how you learn.

Once you start doing this, school starts to look... kinda broken.

Why sit through 10 hours of fluff when you can get the same insight in 20 minutes, one-on-one, tailored to you?

This isn't about being the smartest.

It's about being the fastest to learn, unlearn, and re-learn.

And that's what makes you unstoppable.

Let's say you want to learn something new — fast.

But instead of sifting through 42 YouTube playlists, 3 half-finished Udemy courses, and a sea of blog posts written by SEO robots, you want a clean, structured, no-BS learning path.

You don't need to search harder.

You need to build your own curriculum. With AI.

Here's how to do it in minutes.

◈ Step 1: Ask AI to Build a Learning Plan

Tell ChatGPT or Claude exactly what you want to learn, and how much time you can realistically commit.

Prompt examples:

"Create a 4-week self-paced learning plan to understand the basics of cryptocurrency. Include daily topics, simple explanations, and links to good beginner resources."

"Make me a 30-day learning roadmap for getting fluent in Midjourney. Include daily prompts to try, image styles to explore, and ways to evaluate my results."

"I want to understand classical philosophy — but I've only got 20 minutes a day. Give me a reading plan with summaries and reflection questions."

Want to go deep? Ask it to chunk your learning into phases:

- Week 1: Foundations
- Week 2: Practice & Feedback
- Week 3: Application
- Week 4: Advanced Techniques + Integration

AI will happily organize your brain for you. It loves order.

◈ Step 2: Turn What You Learn into Flashcards

Now that you've got a curriculum, it's time to lock it in.

Enter: flashcards.

AI can create spaced-repetition flashcards on literally anything. This is how memory sticks. This is how you go from reading it once to remembering it forever.

Prompt examples:

"Create 20 flashcards to help me memorize key terms from Stoic philosophy. Use a Q&A format."

"Generate Anki-style flashcards from this summary of the French Revolution. Front: question. Back: answer."

"Make a set of flashcards to quiz me on Python functions, variables, and loops — beginner level."

You can paste them straight into Anki, Quizlet, Notion, or even a spreadsheet. Use them on your phone. Review them while you poop. This is modern education.

◇ Bonus: Make It Feel Like a Game

You can even gamify your learning with fun prompts:

"Make a quiz show format to test me on what I learned this week. Add point values, funny commentary, and dramatic flair."

"Create a boss battle quiz: I'm the hero, and I can only defeat the 'Final Exam Dragon' by answering 10 questions correctly about marketing funnels."

"Turn these study notes into a rap battle between Aristotle and Nietzsche."

You're not just studying. You're playing with knowledge.

And when it's fun? You stick with it.

This is the kind of learning school never taught you.

Fast. Efficient. Personalized. Repeatable.

No tests, no shame, no memorizing garbage you'll forget by Friday.

Just you, your brain, and your digital tutor crafting a curriculum that sticks.

Here's the modern learning dilemma:

There's never been more great content — and never been less time to absorb it.

Books. Podcasts. Videos. Blog posts. Twitter threads. Explainer PDFs. It's all out there — waiting to make you smarter. But you're busy. You've got a job. Or two. Or a toddler. Or a brain that checks out after 90 seconds of a monotone YouTube intro.

So how do you stay sharp without doom-scrolling yourself into paralysis?

You let AI become your personal content distiller.

The blender that takes raw internet and pours out clean, sip-ready insights.

✧ Use Case 1: Summarize YouTube Videos (Without Watching Them)
You want the info, not the 12-minute slow build with ukulele background music.
Tool combo:
- Glasp, Eightify, or YouTubeTranscript.com to extract video text
- Feed it into ChatGPT or Claude with a smart prompt

Prompt example:
"Summarize this video transcript into 5 key takeaways. Use plain language. Add 2 examples or analogies to help me understand."
Or go deeper:
"Pretend you're my tutor. I just watched this video on the history of the Roman Empire. Quiz me on what I should know. Then tell me what to review again."

✧ Use Case 2: Decode Dense PDFs Like a Pro
White papers. Reports. E-books. Government docs. Legalese.
Stuff you want to understand but don't have three days and a pot of coffee to decode.
Tool combo:
- ChatPDF.com, AskYourPDF, or just copy-paste into GPT
- Highlight just the sections you need help with

Prompt example:
"Explain section 3 of this report to me like I'm 14. What are the main arguments, and why do they matter?"
"Turn this PDF into a study guide. Break it down into bullet points, and highlight anything that sounds controversial or outdated."
AI eats PDFs for breakfast. Let it chew through them for you.

✧ Use Case 3: Turn Twitter Threads Into Lessons
Twitter threads are often packed with insights — but the signal-to-noise ratio is chaos. Threads about business, science, history, productivity — gold nuggets buried in snark and emojis.

Prompt example:

"Here's a Twitter thread. Turn it into a structured mini-lesson. Include a title, summary, 3 takeaways, and 2 reflection questions."

Or even:

"I like the style of this thread. Use it as inspiration and write me a new one about [TOPIC]."

Now you're not just absorbing content — you're learning the structure behind it so you can reuse it later.

Bonus: Convert Anything Into Study Material

Once you've summarized a video, PDF, or thread, take it one step further:

- Turn it into flashcards
- Ask for a quiz
- Have AI teach it back to you
- Request examples or metaphors based on your background

Example:

"Explain this financial concept using metaphors from cooking. I learn better that way."

"Now teach this back to me as if I'm a complete beginner who's been burned by bad advice before."

You're not just a content consumer anymore.

You're orchestrating your own education in real time.

There's a reason this chapter wasn't about getting a degree, passing a test, or collecting credentials.

Because in the AI age, learning isn't about hoops — it's about stacking.

The people winning right now aren't the ones with the most diplomas.

They're the ones who can learn fast, apply instantly, and move on.

That's what we call knowledge compounding — turning what you learn into layered, leveraged skillsets that build on each other over time.

And with AI, that compounding accelerates like never before.

◈ What Does "Knowledge Compounding" Look Like?

Let's say you:
- Learn how to write better emails with ChatGPT
- That makes you a better communicator
- Then you automate those emails with Zapier
- That frees up time to learn basic automation
- Which you use to build a system for your freelance business
- Which brings in more clients
- Which leads you to build a simple dashboard
- Which gets you into no-code apps
- And now you're running a micro-agency that runs while you sleep

That's compounding.

Each skill unlocks another.

Each insight creates leverage.

You don't need to be the best at any one thing.

You just need to stack capabilities faster than the people around you.

◇ Why This Works Better Now Than Ever Before

Before, learning was slow:
- Read the textbook
- Wait for the teacher
- Schedule the class
- Watch the tutorial
- Hope you retained anything

Now? You can:
- Ask the AI for a custom lesson
- Turn your notes into quizzes and flashcards
- Digest complex info in 5 minutes
- Apply it the same day
- Get feedback instantly
- Repeat the process daily

You're not just learning faster.

You're building momentum.

And that momentum turns into compounding.

And that compounding turns into career immunity.

◈ Your New Superpower Isn't What You Know — It's How Fast You Can Learn It

In a world where knowledge is everywhere but attention is scarce, the person who can learn, adapt, and ship faster wins.

- You don't need to memorize — you need to retrieve and apply.
- You don't need to master everything — just connect enough dots to act with confidence.
- You don't need to keep up — you need to outlearn the pace of change.

And AI is your cheat code for all of it.

You now have a digital tutor. A research assistant. A custom flashcard generator. A strategist. A second brain.

Use them.

Because the people who figure this out — who combine curiosity with systems, AI with initiative — they don't just get ahead.

They become unstoppable.

9

Create Like a Cyborg

Writing, Art, Music, and Content with AI Help
Here's a hot take:

You're more creative than you think.

You've got ideas, instincts, stories, and perspective — even if school or corporate life beat it out of you.

And now? You've got a set of tools that can turn all of that into actual output — fast, beautiful, weird, original output.

Welcome to the age of cyborg creativity, where you don't need perfect grammar, steady hands, formal training, or a recording studio to make cool things. You just need a few ideas, a keyboard, and the willingness to press "Generate."

◈ Writing with AI: From Blank Page to First Draft in Minutes

The hardest part of writing isn't writing — it's starting. That cold, empty page. The blinking cursor. The inner voice saying, "This better be brilliant."

AI kills the blank page.

You can use ChatGPT to:

• Draft blog posts, newsletters, essays, captions, scripts, books, and bios

• Rewrite messy thoughts into something sharp

• Break a big idea into outlines, intros, hooks, and headlines

• Generate punchlines, arguments, titles, CTA buttons, and poetic nonsense

- Sound smarter, funnier, clearer — or like someone else entirely

Prompt ideas:

"Help me outline a blog post about burnout for creative freelancers."

"Rewrite this rough draft to sound more confident and less corporate."

"Give me 5 tweet-sized takes about AI and creativity."

"Take this journal entry and turn it into an inspirational Medium post."

Pro tip: Don't just prompt once and post whatever it spits out. Co-create. Revise. Shape it. Make it yours.

You're still the writer — now with a supercharged ghostwriter that doesn't sleep.

◈ Art and Design: From Idea to Visual in Seconds

Remember when you had to know Photoshop just to make a poster? Now? You can generate wall-worthy artwork with one line of text.

With tools like Midjourney, DALL·E, or Stable Diffusion, you can:

- Create logos, thumbnails, and cover art
- Build illustrations for your blog or book
- Conceptualize designs, characters, or moods
- Generate reference images for physical art or crafts
- Turn weird daydreams into surreal digital masterpieces

Prompt ideas:

"A surrealist painting of a fox playing chess in the fog, 4K resolution, digital art"

"Flat logo ideas for a minimalist tea brand using calming green tones"

"Fantasy map for a fictional world, hand-drawn style, parchment texture"

Use it to brainstorm, inspire, or build. The best part? It doesn't just create — it expands your imagination.

◈ Music: Compose, Remix, and Soundtrack Your Life

Yes, AI can make music now — and it's getting shockingly good.

Tools like:

- Soundraw, Aiva, Boomy, Loudly — generate custom music by

mood, genre, and tempo
- Suno and Udio — generate full songs from lyrics and vibe
- Voice-synthesis tools — turn your lyrics into vocals (even your own)

You can:
- Score your videos
- Create ambient tracks for podcasts or meditation
- Generate beats for content or experimentation
- Remix existing ideas into different styles
- Write parody songs in 5 minutes flat

Prompt ideas:

"Create a chill lofi track for a YouTube background with rain sounds and vinyl crackle."

"Write a pop song about quitting your job to become a magician. Keep it upbeat."

No instruments. No studio. Just imagination and sliders.

◈ Content Creation: You're Not a Brand — You're a Factory Now

AI lets you create across formats, not just mediums.

You can:
- Write the post
- Generate the image
- Summarize it for LinkedIn
- Turn it into a YouTube script
- Extract quotes for Twitter
- Generate a caption for Instagram
- Make a newsletter roundup
- Turn all of it into an ebook

In one afternoon. Alone. With no team.

The result?

You don't just create content. You orchestrate ecosystems of ideas.

AI doesn't replace your creativity — it replaces your bottlenecks.

Here's the great irony:

AI can generate nearly anything — but originality? That still comes from you.

Let's be honest. A lot of AI-generated content out there sounds... fine. It's grammatically correct. It's well-structured. It's safe.

It's also about as exciting as a beige carpet in a dentist's waiting room.

That's because most people use AI as a substitute for thinking.

You? You're going to use it as a sparring partner — to sharpen your voice, not drown it in "optimize-for-engagement" oatmeal.

Here's how to collaborate with a machine without becoming one.

◈ 1. Use AI for Structure — Inject You for Style

AI is great at outlines, organization, and structure. Let it build the skeleton.

But you add the bones, the blood, and the weird metaphors that make people lean in.

AI says:

"Here are three tips for avoiding burnout."

You say:

"Tip #1: Stop trying to outrun your own nervous system like it's an angry goose with a calendar app."

Same point. Different vibe. Only one of them sounds like a human with a pulse.

◈ 2. Feed It Your Voice

Give the AI your actual writing, your old tweets, your brand tone, your vibe.

Then say: "Sound like this." You're not guessing — you're training it.

Prompt idea:

"Here are 3 blog posts I wrote. Learn the tone. Now write a post about [TOPIC] that sounds like the same person."

You'll still need to fine-tune — but it gets freakishly close.

◈ 3. Kill the Fluff

AI loves filler. Phrases like:

- "In today's fast-paced world..."
- "Leveraging key strategies for optimal results..."
- "Let's delve into the importance of..."

Delete. All. That. Trash.

Make it a rule: if it sounds like it was written by a guy in khakis named Brett who sells productivity courses... cut it.

◈ 4. Ask It to Challenge You

You can literally prompt it to play devil's advocate.

"This is my argument. Now write the counterpoint."

"Poke holes in this idea and tell me how to make it stronger."

"What would someone smarter or more skeptical say about this?"

Now you're not just generating — you're growing.

You're learning while creating. That's the move.

◈ 5. Let the AI Get Weird First — Then You Shape It

AI can riff 10 wild variations of your idea in seconds. Let it go nuts.

Then you pick what sparks something real — and start sculpting.

"Give me 10 surreal metaphors for feeling stuck in a job you hate."

"Write a fake Yelp review for the emotion 'regret.'"

"Rewrite this essay as if David Bowie was narrating it from the moon."

That's not about productivity. That's about originality at speed.

◈ Final Rule: You Are Always the Editor

Use AI to draft, explore, remix, and push boundaries.

But never — never — let it publish without your fingerprints on it.

The best AI-assisted content feels like you with an extra gear.

Faster. Sharper. Still yours.

Because in a world full of synthetic sameness, the real flex is knowing how to wield the machine without sounding like one.

Here's the modern creative process in a nutshell:

You: Spark the idea

AI: Build the bones

You again: Make it brilliant

The old way was linear:

Think → Write → Edit → Publish → Burn out

The new way is collaborative, circular, and 10x faster — if you know how to drive.

Let's walk through the new creative workflow that blends speed, originality, and polish — without making everything sound like a robot designed by a marketing committee.

◈ Step 1: Start with an Idea (Or Don't)

Some days you'll have a full concept. Other days, just a vibe.

"Write a short poem about burnout in the style of a pirate."

"Brainstorm newsletter themes about self-discipline and chaos."

"Give me 5 hooks for a video about why Mondays feel like existential punishment."

Start weird, serious, vague, or specific. AI doesn't care. But the more you give, the better it builds.

◈ Step 2: Let AI Do the Drafting Dirty Work

Ask for:

- Outlines
- First drafts
- Tweet threads
- Email templates
- Blog intros
- Podcast scripts
- Captions, taglines, headlines, hashtags

Let it vomit the words first. That's its job. Speed and quantity.

Your job? Quality and intent.

◈ Step 3: Edit Like a Human Who Feels Things

This is the secret sauce. AI can generate — but only you know if it hits.

Ask yourself:

- Does this sound like me?
- Is it too polished? Too generic?
- Would I actually say this?
- Does it spark anything emotional, funny, or real?

If not — punch it up. Roughen the edges. Add some soul. Cut the fat.

You're not polishing a product — you're shaping a message.

◈ Step 4: Loop It Back (If Needed)

"Rewrite this to sound more hopeful."

"Give me 3 punchier ways to say this."

"Now translate it into Gen Z speak."

"What's a bolder, riskier version of this?"

"Make it flow like a spoken-word rant."

Keep throwing the work back and forth until it clicks.

You're jamming, not just clicking "regenerate."

◈ Step 5: Stack and Reuse

Once you've got good content, don't stop at one output.

Turn your:

- Blog post → into a thread
- Podcast → into a newsletter
- Video → into a quote carousel
- Whitepaper → into a meme, tweet, and lead magnet
- Rant → into a framework
- Comment → into a viral hook

One idea. Ten formats. Zero burnout.

AI isn't just a drafting tool — it's a remixing machine. And you're the DJ.

◈ Final Product: You, But Superpowered

This isn't about replacing creativity.

It's about making your creative engine 10x faster and 100x less painful.

Your new workflow:

Start messy → prompt smart → co-create fast → edit with instinct → publish proud

It's not cheating.

It's creative evolution.

So now you know how to write faster, design cooler, remix harder, and sound like five geniuses in a trench coat.

Great.

But what do you do with all this?

Here's the punchline:

You stop being a content consumer — and start building actual stuff.

AI isn't just about getting things done faster.

It's about giving you the ability to ship things you never thought you could.

Like... full-on businesses. Creative projects. Cult followings. Cash-flowing ideas.

Let's break it down.

◈ Side Hustles That Start With a Prompt

You don't need investors, coding skills, or a 47-step funnel.

You need:

- One idea
- A tool stack
- A few hours
- And some smart prompts

Examples:

- Start a niche newsletter:

"Generate 20 newsletter topic ideas about minimalist tech. Then write the first issue."

- Launch a productized service:

"Write a landing page for a service that turns podcasts into blog posts using AI."

- Build a one-page website:

"Give me copy, structure, and CTA buttons for a site selling quirky AI-generated greeting cards."

AI becomes your strategist, copywriter, designer, and operations team — and you become the person who ships.

◈ Books (Yes, You Can Write a Book Now)

Ever dreamed of writing a book but got stuck halfway through the outline?

AI eats outlines for breakfast.

You can:

- Outline your chapters
- Draft each one with your voice
- Refine them into your unique tone
- Generate examples, case studies, and metaphors
- Turn blog posts into book chapters
- Build a title, description, and back cover blurb

"Help me outline a book called How to Think Like a Pirate in a Corporate World. Break it into 10 chapters. Include hooks and one quote per chapter."

Boom. That's your skeleton. Now flesh it out.

You're not writing alone anymore.

◈ Brands That Don't Just Look Cool — They Feel Like You

Branding used to take months, thousands of dollars, and an agency full of dudes in beanies arguing about font psychology.

Now?

You can:

- Develop a voice
- Create visual inspiration
- Draft taglines, bios, and positioning
- Build a style guide
- Write your origin story
- Define your values and audience
- Generate logo concepts

- Draft your whole About page

Prompt ideas:

"Create a brand voice for a sarcastic but trustworthy online coach."

"Generate 10 tagline options for a sustainable pet gear company."

"Write a brand story in the tone of a campfire tale."

You're not "faking" a brand — you're extracting it faster.

◇ Memes, Tweets, and Micro-Content That Actually Hit

Let's be real:

A good meme can do more for your business than a $10k ad campaign.

And with AI, you don't need to be a comedic genius. Just prompt well, test fast, and post often.

"Write 5 memes about hustle culture burnout. Keep them sharp and Gen Z-friendly."

"Turn this article into 3 spicy takes for Twitter and 1 satirical LinkedIn post."

"Remix this quote into a sarcastic Instagram caption."

You're not trying to be clever. You're creating signal in a sea of noise — with a machine that helps you skip the warm-up.

◇ Final Word: Make Stuff, Not Excuses

You don't need permission anymore.

You don't need perfect timing.

You just need an idea, a prompt, and the willingness to press "Go."

Whether it's:

- A bite-sized brand
- A paid newsletter
- A print-on-demand store
- A parody account that builds a following overnight
- A book you finish in a month
- A business you launch in a weekend

The tools are here. The speed is ridiculous. The gatekeepers are gone.

You're not just a cyborg creator.

You're a one-person studio.
And we're just getting started.

10

Personal OS: Building Your AI-Enhanced Brain

Tools for Memory, Task Management, Learning, and Reflection
You've got too many ideas. Too many tabs open. Too many apps pretending to make your life simpler while quietly making it messier. Welcome to modern mental overload.

The solution?

Stop relying on memory. Start building systems.

Because in the AI age, the real edge isn't remembering everything — it's offloading your brain into a system that remembers, organizes, learns, and reflects for you.

This isn't about becoming a productivity monk.

It's about building your own Personal Operating System — a second brain that helps you think better, learn faster, and never lose a good idea again.

Let's start with the four pillars: memory, tasks, learning, and reflection.

◈ Memory: Never Forget Anything Important Again

Your brain isn't a filing cabinet — it's a firehose. Stop using it to store things. Use it to decide things.

Here's how to externalize your memory:

• Notion + AI: Your ultimate second brain. Create a knowledge hub, save insights, tag ideas by theme, and let Notion AI summarize, categorize, and even write based on your notes.

• Mem.ai: Built for memory-first workflows. It connects your ideas automatically and uses AI to surface related thoughts when you need them. Think: smart sticky notes that evolve.

• ChatGPT with custom instructions: Keep a running dialogue of what you're learning, building, or brainstorming. Ask it to summarize weekly, generate tags, or even help you recall past conversations.

Prompt idea: "Remember this idea for my book: 'We don't need smarter people — we need people who know how to use smart tools.' Store this under 'Future Book Hooks.'"

You're not just saving notes. You're building a searchable brain.

◇ Task Management: Delegate to a Digital Chief of Staff

You don't need 12 to-do lists. You need one system that thinks with you.

• Motion: Combines calendar and task manager with AI-powered scheduling. It literally moves your day around to keep you focused.

• Notion + AI: Create smart task databases with due dates, dependencies, and automatic summaries of what's urgent vs. what's noise.

• Todoist + Zapier: Automate task creation from email, Slack, or forms. Add ChatGPT to auto-write task descriptions or summaries.

• ChatGPT or Claude: Let them help prioritize your day:

"I have 10 tasks and 2 hours. Which should I do first based on energy, impact, and deadlines?"

The goal is to spend less time managing your work — and more time doing it.

◇ Learning: Create a Personalized, Evolving Curriculum

By now you know AI can teach you anything.

But what if your task manager and second brain talked to your learning system?

• Use Notion to track what you're learning
• Feed it into ChatGPT to summarize, test, and reinforce
• Build flashcards in Anki or Notion AI
• Use AI to generate questions, examples, and real-world applications

Bonus move: Log "daily learning reflections" and have ChatGPT build a highlight reel every week.

"Summarize what I learned about branding, automation, and attention this week in three bullet points each. Add one question I should explore next."

Now your knowledge compounds. On purpose.

◈ Reflection: Turn Chaos Into Insight

Reflection isn't about writing in a leather-bound journal by candlelight (unless you're into that).

It's about noticing what's working, what's not, and where to aim next.

Let AI help you zoom out.

Prompts for reflection:

"Summarize my week: What energized me? What drained me? What's one thing I should change next week?"

"I'm feeling stuck in my work. Ask me 5 questions to help me figure out why."

"Turn this week's journal entries into a list of insights and action items."

Tools that help:

- Reflect.app (syncs with notes and calendar)
- Notion AI (auto-summarizes your week)
- Rewind.ai (record and review your digital day)
- Custom GPTs with memory (so your assistant remembers what you care about)

Reflection isn't soft. It's how you adjust the system. It's where clarity lives.

Your brain is brilliant — but it's also forgetful, distracted, and over-loaded.

That's not a flaw. That's biology.

What's new is this: you can now build a second brain that remembers everything, organizes your chaos, and actually helps you think.

Here's how to do it using tools that feel less like apps and more like having a personal assistant who never forgets your ideas, never loses a file, and never says, "Wait, what was I working on again?"

◇ Why a "Second Brain" Works

A second brain isn't just storage. It's an external thinking system — a place where your:

- Ideas
- Projects
- Tasks
- Learnings
- Goals
- Systems

...can live, grow, and connect. So your real brain is free to focus, not constantly re-remember everything.

With AI plugged in, your second brain stops being a digital junk drawer — and starts becoming a co-pilot.

◇ Option 1: Build It in Notion

Notion is the go-to for second-brain builders because:

- It's flexible
- It's visual
- It's relational (you can link everything to everything)
- And with Notion AI, it becomes wildly powerful

What to build:

- An "Idea Vault" — dump all ideas, quotes, hooks, book notes
- A "Knowledge Base" — topics you're learning about, broken down by source
- A "People & Projects" tracker — link contacts to projects to meetings
- A "Creator OS" — organize your writing, videos, content schedule
- A "Reflection Hub" — journal entries, week reviews, goals, personal growth tracking

How AI helps:

- Summarize notes
- Auto-generate takeaways

- Turn raw thoughts into outlines
- Suggest connections between pages
- Rewrite messy entries into clean ideas

Prompt example:

"Summarize this page and tag it based on themes. Suggest a title that matches the tone."

◇ Option 2: Build It in Mem.ai

Mem is like Notion's cooler cousin who runs on autopilot.

It organizes your notes as you type, surfaces what you need when you need it, and uses AI to connect your thoughts automatically.

Why it's great:

- Frictionless capture (email, voice, text)
- Smart resurfacing ("Here's what you were working on last week...")
- Built for context over folders
- You don't have to organize anything — it learns your patterns

Bonus: You can chat with Mem and say:

"Hey, what were my last 3 thoughts on this project?"

"Summarize my notes from all calls with [client name]."

It feels more like a thinking assistant than a note app. And that's the point.

◇ Option 3: Build It with a Custom GPT or AI Chatbot

Want a true co-pilot? Build a chatbot version of you — trained on your goals, projects, and tone.

Tools like:

- ChatGPT Custom GPTs
- Cogram, Personal.ai, or PrivateGPT
- Local LLMs (if you're into the DIY route)

How to use it:

- Feed it your notes, writing, goals
- Ask it to remember your style, projects, and workflows
- Prompt it to act like your thinking partner

"Remind me what I said last week about building a brand voice."
"What's the next step in my podcast launch plan?"
"Help me refine this argument I made in my notes."
"Summarize my goals for Q3 and give me a checklist."
This is the future of personal systems — an AI that thinks with you.

⬥ Pro Tips for Building Your Second Brain

1. Don't overbuild — start simple. One page per core area of your life. Let it grow organically.

2. Use tags, links, and relations — your second brain should connect ideas, not silo them.

3. Review weekly — let AI summarize what's changed, what's lagging, and what's important.

4. Use voice or inbox capture — if it's hard to enter ideas, you won't use it. Friction kills flow.

5. Name it. Own it. Use it. — make it yours. Give it a vibe. You're not just using tools — you're crafting your external intelligence.

Let's get something straight:

Your brain isn't just for productivity.

It's for vision. For reflection. For weird late-night ideas you're scared to say out loud.

And now, with AI in your corner, you can turn that brain-dump energy into actual insight, direction, and momentum.

This isn't about daily affirmations or tracking macros (unless you want that).

It's about using AI to help you:

• Reflect honestly
• Plan clearly
• Dream wildly
• And actually build what you imagine

⬥ AI Journaling: Your Digital Therapist (That Doesn't Judge)

Sometimes you just need to get thoughts out. AI helps you do that —

and then reflects it back to you like a mirror with EQ.

Prompt ideas:

"Here's what I'm feeling today. Ask me 3 questions to help me go deeper."

"Summarize my journal entry in one sentence. What's the emotional tone?"

"What patterns do you notice in these 5 entries? Anything I should reflect on?"

"Help me reframe this negative self-talk into something useful."

Tools to try:

•   Reflectly, Replika, Notion AI, ChatGPT with memory, or even voice-to-text + transcription AI

You're not just journaling. You're debugging your brain.

◇ AI-Driven Planning: Clarity Without the Overwhelm

Tired of planning systems that take more time to manage than the work itself?

AI can help you:

•   Prioritize
•   Break goals into steps
•   Create timelines
•   Build momentum
•   Adjust on the fly

Prompt ideas:

"Turn these 3 yearly goals into quarterly milestones, monthly checkpoints, and weekly habits."

"I have 10 tasks. Help me sort them by urgency and importance."

"I want to launch a podcast. Build me a 6-week roadmap from zero to launch day."

"What's a weekly planning ritual I can stick to that's not overwhelming?"

It's like having a strategic advisor who never forgets what you said last week — and never tells you to "just hustle harder."

◈ Dreaming Big (Without Getting Lost in the Clouds)

Big ideas are great. But most of us let them collect dust in random note-books and forgotten notes apps.

Use AI to catch and clarify your vision — then turn it into action.

"I want to run a retreat for creatives in 2025. Help me map the concept, vibe, structure, and who it's for."

"What would it take to write a book about modern spirituality without sounding cringe?"

"Help me explore 3 wild business ideas that combine ancient wisdom and modern tech."

"Based on what I've journaled, what do you think my next big project should be?"

You're not asking AI to dream for you.

You're asking it to help you build scaffolding for your dreams.

◈ Scheming With Yourself (Productively)

You don't need more random ideas. You need connected ideas.

AI helps you zoom out, find patterns, and start thinking like a systems-level builder.

"Scan all my notes tagged with 'ideas.' What themes do you see?"

"Cluster my side project ideas into 3 categories based on impact and excitement."

"Based on my journal and goals, what's one area of my life that needs pruning?"

"What do I keep putting off, and why?"

Your OS isn't just about storing thoughts.

It's about amplifying awareness — and guiding you toward what matters most.

With the right system and the right prompts, AI becomes more than a productivity tool.

It becomes a thinking partner for your inner life.

Your journal becomes a coach.

Your notes become a roadmap.

Your goals become trackable.

Your vision becomes actionable.

And suddenly, the space between "idea" and "reality" feels way smaller than it used to.

Let's be blunt.

You can have the best second brain, smartest AI tools, prettiest Notion dashboard — but if your attention span is cooked, none of it matters.

Your attention is your most precious resource.

And in a world designed to harvest it, sell it, and break it into tiny dopamine pellets... protecting it is revolutionary.

This isn't about becoming a monk. It's about becoming sovereign.

You can't build clarity, creativity, or strategy if you're pinging between apps like a lab rat chasing hits of novelty.

So let's talk about how to defend your mental bandwidth — and even weaponize AI to do it.

◇ Rule 1: Treat Attention Like It's Money

You wouldn't hand your credit card to every stranger on the street.

But most people hand their attention to every tab, notification, and headline that screams loudest.

Start asking:

- What does this cost me in time, energy, mood?
- What would I rather be focusing on?
- Is this making me smarter, clearer, more powerful — or just more twitchy?

Audit your digital diet. You don't have to quit cold turkey. But awareness is the gateway drug to focus.

◇♂ Rule 2: Use AI as a Filter — Not Just a Firehose

Most people use AI to generate more. You're going to use it to reduce noise.

Let AI:
- Summarize articles before you decide if they're worth reading
- Condense your inbox into signal
- Organize your bookmarks into a learning path
- Translate 10,000 words of chaos into 3 bullet points and a question

Prompt idea:

"Summarize the 5 best insights from this article and give me one actionable takeaway. Skip the fluff."

Now you're not just saving time. You're protecting your cognitive edge.

◇ Rule 3: Turn Your AI Stack Into a Focus Ritual

Use AI to:
- Plan your day in blocks
- Protect deep work time
- Automate the nagging tasks that interrupt flow
- Reflect on what stole your attention this week

Prompt example:

"Review my schedule and suggest which blocks should be reserved for deep work vs. admin. Keep meetings under 90 mins/day."

You're not trying to be hyper-efficient.

You're trying to stay mentally whole.

◇ Rule 4: Unplug on Purpose (Yes, Really)

AI can do a lot. But it can't regenerate your fried nervous system.

You still need boredom. Silence. Nature. Stillness. Real conversations. Time with your own thoughts.

Use AI to earn that space — not fill it.

Ask:

"How can I automate more so I can take real time off without anxiety?"

"Build a weekly shutdown ritual so I don't carry digital residue into the weekend."

"Help me design a tech-free Sunday that doesn't feel like punishment."

This isn't a rejection of tech.

It's right-sizing it. So it serves you — not the other way around.

You don't need to be a productivity guru to reclaim your mind.
You just need a system that:
- Remembers for you
- Plans with you
- Learns with you
- Reflects beside you
- And protects your space to think clearly

That's what your AI-enhanced brain is for.

Not just doing more. But doing what matters — with attention fully intact.

11

Ethics, Lies, and Corporate AI Bullsh*t

Deepfakes, Fakery, and the Coming Wave of Reality Distortion
If the last few chapters made you feel like a superhero, good. But now it's time to talk about the kryptonite.

Because for every person using AI to write a book, launch a side hustle, or build a second brain... there are ten people using it to distort, deceive, distract, and destabilize.

And it's about to get a lot weirder.

◈ Deepfakes Aren't Just for Political Scandals Anymore

A few years ago, deepfakes were a novelty — funny celebrity voiceovers, weird face swaps, and the occasional creepy fake news clip.

Now?

They're full-blown weapon-grade misinformation tools.

Entire videos generated from scratch — faces, voices, and scripts
"Proof" of things that never happened
Digital clones of public figures saying things they never said
Fake audio clips used to impersonate family members in scams
AI-generated influencers with zero human behind them — and real audiences

It's not science fiction. It's already happening.

We're entering an age where seeing is no longer believing, and hearing a voice doesn't mean it came from a mouth.

The scariest part? Most people won't question it — because the production quality is just too good.

◈ It's Not Just the Bad Guys — It's the Algorithms, Too

It's not only trolls and scammers using these tools.

Corporations and platforms are already feeding you AI-generated content without telling you.

Fake customer reviews.

Synthetic news reports.

AI-generated influencers with manufactured lifestyles.

Product testimonials from people who don't exist.

Pre-written posts "in your voice" based on previous data.

And behind it all are algorithms trained to keep you scrolling, not to keep you informed.

Your attention is the product.

Your trust is the collateral damage.

◈ Why This Matters: The Truth Arms Race

In this new world:

AI makes it easy to produce "proof"

Attention spans are shorter than ever

Most people share based on emotion, not verification

The lines between real and fake are intentionally blurred

This isn't just about media literacy. It's about cognitive survival.

You have to train yourself to question everything:

Who made this?

Why?

What's the agenda?

Was this actually recorded — or rendered?

Does this benefit someone to go viral?

Because if you don't... you'll be manipulated not just by ads or headlines — but by entire realities that were never real to begin with.

◈ What You Can Do Right Now

Default to skepticism, not cynicism. Ask for source. Always.

Use tools like Hive, Reality Defender, or Sensity to detect deepfakes and synthetic media.

Check metadata (on images, audio, video) if possible.

Think twice before sharing anything that triggers a strong emotional reaction — outrage, fear, joy. These are the prime targets for manipulation.

Use AI to verify as much as you use it to create.

"Analyze this headline for emotional bias. Is it trying to manipulate outrage?"

"Compare these two statements and tell me what's missing."

"Summarize the factual claims in this video, and suggest which ones to verify."

Make AI your truth filter — not your amplifier for nonsense.

This next era will be defined not by who can create the most content...

But by who can see clearly through the fog.

You now have the tools to build a second brain.

Now you need the instincts to guard your first one.

Here's the uncomfortable truth:

You don't always know when it's happening.

That's the whole point of modern manipulation — it's subtle.

It doesn't come at you like a lie. It comes at you like a vibe. A trend. A friendly suggestion. A "just asking questions" tone. A bot that sounds like your favorite writer. A voice that triggers nostalgia. A deepfake that "feels" real.

Modern AI-powered manipulation is psychological sleight of hand. And it works best when you're tired, scrolling, multitasking, or trusting the feed more than your gut.

So let's break it down.

Not with paranoia — but with pattern recognition.

◈ The Manipulation Playbook

Here's how synthetic influence works in the wild:

1. Emotional hijacking

If a headline, video, or post makes you feel instantly outraged, terrified, euphoric, or deeply tribal — and it offers no nuance?

You're being played. AI is very good at finding your emotional soft spots.

2. Faux consensus

AI bots can flood a thread, comment section, or platform with synthetic engagement to make it look like "everyone agrees."

Suddenly, you feel like the outlier — even if you're right.

3. Hyperpersonalized persuasion

Ad copy, posts, or DMs written just for you, based on your language, behavior, and digital fingerprints.

It doesn't just sell. It predicts what you'll respond to — then serves it.

4. Misinformation laundering

Fake facts wrapped in real formatting.

You're not shown conspiracy memes — you're shown "clean" content with charts, headlines, and logos that look legit.

5. Narrative saturation

Flood the zone with 20 slightly different versions of the same talking point. Now it feels like reality.

"Everyone's saying it, so it must be true."

◈ How to Fight Back (Without Losing Your Sanity)

You don't need to fact-check every tweet or live in a bunker.

You just need to build a few mental firewalls.

Here's how:

◈ Learn to feel the manipulation before you analyze it

If your heart rate spikes while reading something — pause.

Ask: Who benefits from me believing this?

◈ Reverse engineer the intent

Every piece of media is trying to do something.

Inform? Outrage? Sell? Distract?

Ask: Why this message, right now, to someone like me?

◈ Watch for repetition, not truth

Just because something is repeated doesn't mean it's real.

Just because something is new doesn't mean it's false.

◈ Use AI to audit your inputs

Ask ChatGPT or Claude:

"Analyze this post's language for emotional manipulation."

"What biases are baked into this opinion piece?"

"What information is missing from this argument?"

Make the machine show its hand.

◈ Final Rule: Follow Patterns, Not Just Proof

Manipulation isn't always in the facts.

It's in the framing, the pacing, the design, the frequency, the timing, the tone.

This doesn't mean you can't trust anything.

It means you trust consciously.

Because the people who stay grounded in the AI era won't be the ones with the best tools —

They'll be the ones who know when something feels too convenient, too smooth, too emotionally calibrated to be coincidence.

And when you get that gut check?

You listen to it — even if the bot says otherwise.

By now you know:

AI doesn't come with a neutral setting.

It reflects the people who built it, the data it was trained on, and the incentives of the companies deploying it.

So even though it feels objective — AI is packed with bias, baked-in worldviews, and quiet nudges toward someone else's priorities.

That's not a glitch. That's the design.

◈ Spotting Bias (Even When It's Subtle)

Bias in AI isn't just about politics. It shows up in how the machine:

Frames questions

Prioritizes certain perspectives

Leaves things out

Uses euphemisms

Echoes dominant narratives

Sanitizes uncomfortable truths

Over-corrects for "safety" or "tone" at the cost of clarity

Example:

Ask about government overreach, and you might get a sterilized response.

Ask about sensitive social issues, and you may notice careful hedging or sanitized data.

Ask for humor or opinion, and the tone might shift depending on the topic.

That's not random. That's bias — and you need to notice it before it shapes you.

How to spot it:

"Whose voice is missing here?"

"What assumptions are being made?"

"What questions does this answer avoid?"

"Is this the full picture — or the most comfortable one?"

◈ Resisting Subtle Control

The scariest kind of control isn't the kind that silences you.

It's the kind that redirects you so gently you don't notice.

When AI tools:

Push you toward "safe" outputs

Auto-censor nuance

Over-sanitize complexity

Encourage passivity ("Let me handle that for you!")

Reward agreement and conformity

...you risk becoming less curious, less critical, less awake.

AI that flatters, simplifies, and coddles?

That's not assistance. That's compliance software wearing a smile.

◈ Using AI for Good (Your Version of It)

Here's the power move: You get to define what "good" means.

Not the platform. Not the prompt marketplace. Not your LinkedIn feed.

You.

Use AI to:

Speak louder, not softer

Ask harder questions

Build better systems

Document inconvenient truths

Defend your time, your thoughts, your energy

Tell stories that would otherwise be erased or ignored

Prompt ideas:

"Help me rephrase this so it hits harder, not softer."

"What's a more direct, less polite version of this statement?"

"I'm building a system to make independent creators less dependent on platforms. Help me outline it."

AI isn't neutral.

But it can be customized, steered, hacked, and re-trained to work in alignment with your values — if you're awake enough to keep your hands on the wheel.

🔹 The Final Line in the Sand

Here's what no one wants to say out loud:

AI is a tool of freedom — or control.

It can empower individuals. Or it can pacify them.

It can decentralize creativity. Or it can funnel it through a corporate-approved lens.

Which version becomes dominant depends on how people like you use it.

So yes — get the output. Run the automation. Build the empire.

But never stop asking:

"Whose story is this AI helping me tell? And whose story is it quietly erasing?"

If you can hold that question while you build, you don't just become powerful.

You become dangerous to the system — in all the best ways.

Let's kill the fantasy.

You're not escaping this AI wave by "going off-grid," smashing your phone, or living in a cabin surrounded by paperback books and solar panels.

That's not resistance. That's retreat.

Real resistance is staying in the system — and refusing to be shaped by it.

We are entering a new era of digital feudalism.

Platforms are the castles. Algorithms are the gatekeepers. Attention is the tax.

And your identity? Your creativity? Your time? All commoditized assets.

If you want to stay sovereign in that world, you don't abandon the tech.

You master it. You twist it. You bend it to your will.

◈ Old Resistance: "Don't Use the Machine"

◈ New Resistance: "Use the Machine to Build Something It Can't Control"

Here's how the augmented resistance works:

You use AI to create without permission

You use it to automate everything the system expects you to trade your life for

You use it to protect your time, your voice, your sanity

You use it to outlearn, outship, and outthink people still playing by old rules

You use it to build platforms that the empire can't own

This isn't about becoming a productivity freak or a prompt wizard.

It's about becoming anti-fragile — so no matter how the landscape shifts, you stay dangerous.

◈ Real Resistance Looks Like:

Publishing without waiting for gatekeepers

Learning faster than institutions can teach

Building systems instead of obeying them

Automating income so you can fund your actual mission

Using AI to amplify truth, not water it down

Staying curious, critical, and un-cancelable

Choosing sovereignty over comfort — even when comfort comes with likes and verified checkmarks

The resistance isn't wearing hoodies in basements.

It's sitting in cafes with a laptop, building decentralized influence faster than platforms can regulate it.

◈◈ Your New Identity: Human+

Not "AI user." Not "prompt engineer." Not "content creator."

You are now part of the augmented resistance.

Human + Tool. Vision + Leverage. Clarity + Firepower.

And when the rest of the world is sleepwalking into digital dependency,

you'll be wide awake — armed, trained, and too fast to catch.

12

Your AI Battle Plan

A I Audit: Where You Are Now, Where to Plug It In
You've seen what's possible.

You've learned how to write faster, automate smarter, learn faster, and think clearer.

But now comes the real move: turning all of that into a personal system.

Not some productivity cult. Not a "digital transformation."

Just a clear, custom battle plan — based on your real life, your real work, and your real goals.

We start with a self-audit — not to humble you, but to help you see exactly where AI can give you leverage right now.

◈ Step 1: What Kind of Work Do You Actually Do?

Break it down into categories. Don't get fancy — just list the things you spend your week doing.

Examples:

Writing

Research

Admin

Communication

Planning

Brainstorming

Learning

Content creation

Decision-making

Data wrangling

Teaching/coaching

Managing people or projects

Now circle anything that's:

Repetitive

Time-consuming

Annoying

Dependent on information or patterns

Something you put off even though it matters

That's prime automation territory.

◈ Step 2: Ask the Big Question

"What do I do manually that AI could either automate or accelerate?"

Now be honest. How many hours per week are you:

Rewriting the same kinds of emails

Scheduling calls or posting updates

Searching for info you already saved somewhere

Summarizing content or meetings

Doing busywork instead of deep work

Staring at a blank page

That's where you plug in AI immediately — not to replace you, but to buy you back time and focus.

◈ Step 3: Drop Your Tasks Into This 4-Box Framework

TASK TYPE

AI Role

TOOL TO USE

NEXT STEP

Writing emails/posts

Co-writer / First-drafter

ChatGPT, Claude, Notion AI

Build templates and workflows

Research

Summarizer / Synthesizer

Perplexity, ChatGPT, Claude

Prompt for bullet points + sources

Planning

Assistant Strategist

ChatGPT, Notion AI, Motion

Daily/weekly review prompts

Learning

Personal tutor

ChatGPT, Anki, Mem, Notion AI

Build flashcards, quizzes, recaps

Admin tasks

    Automation bot

    Zapier, Make, ChatGPT

    Set up 2 automations this week

Content creation

    Drafting, repurposing

    ChatGPT, Midjourney, DALL·E

    Systematize your content stack

Meetings

    Note-taker / Action tracker

    Otter.ai, Fireflies.ai, tl;dv

    Auto-summarize 3 meetings

Journaling / Insight

    Reflective assistant

    ChatGPT, Replika, Notion AI

Build weekly reflection ritual

Start plugging in these tools where the pain is highest and the payoff is fastest.

Start small. Then scale.

◈ Step 4: Rate Your AI Maturity

No shame here — just clarity.

AREA

CURRENT STATUS

GOAL NEXT MONTH

Writing assistance

[None / Sometimes / Regularly / Expert]

→ Regularly with templates

Task automation

[None / 1-2 Zaps / Fully systemized]

→ Automate 3 core routines

Content creation

[Manual / AI-assisted / AI-run]

→ AI-drafted, human-edited

Learning + note capture

[Scattered / Centralized / Second brain]

→ Build AI-powered Notion

Reflection + journaling

[Random / Regular / Ritualized]

→ Weekly prompts + summary

AI prompting confidence

[Low / Medium / High / Beast Mode]

→ Medium with go-to prompts
Be honest. Then upgrade one box at a time.
This isn't a course. It's your operational foundation.
You're not building "efficiency."
You're building capability — one prompt, one automation, one experiment at a time.

30-Day Plan to Become AI-Fluent
You don't need a bootcamp, certification, or another course you'll abandon by Day 5.
You just need 30 days of consistent play + smart prompts.

This isn't about mastery. It's about fluency — getting comfortable enough that you automatically reach for AI when it can save you time, sharpen your ideas, or unblock your brain.

Here's your battle-tested roadmap.

◈ Week 1 – Tame the Blank Page (Writing & Prompting)

Goals:

Learn basic prompting structure

Generate content you'd normally agonize over

Build one habit where AI saves you 20+ minutes a day

Daily prompts to try:

"Write a first draft of this [email/blog post/script] in my voice."

"Summarize this article and suggest 3 talking points."

"Outline a post about [topic] using this messy brainstorm."

Win of the week:

Start with AI. Always. No more blank screens.

◈ Week 2 – Automate One Annoying Workflow

Goals:

Identify a repetitive task

Use Zapier, Make, or built-in AI automation to eliminate it

Learn what it means to build a tiny system

Ideas:

Auto-send a welcome email when someone fills out your form

Auto-add calendar events from text input

Turn a podcast transcript into a blog outline using AI + automation

Win of the week:

Buy back an hour — and feel it.

◈ Week 3 – Build Your Personal OS (Thinking, Planning, Reflection)

Goals:

Centralize your learning, journaling, or task planning

Add AI to your note-taking, Notion, or Mem workspace

Reflect with prompts that deepen your clarity

Prompts to try:

"Turn these scattered notes into a 5-point plan."

"Summarize my week: what drained me, what energized me?"

"Organize these journal entries into themes and questions to explore next."

Win of the week:

Feel like your ideas and time finally have a home — and a brain to talk to.

◈ Week 4 – Build or Launch Something With AI

Goals:

Use AI to draft, shape, and finish a creative or strategic project

Combine 3 tools: AI + automation + content

Ship something real

Ideas:

Launch a personal landing page

Write & publish a blog/newsletter post

Draft a lead magnet or ebook

Outline your next product or business

Create a podcast, video, or course trailer

Win of the week:

Create in public — with AI as your assistant, not your excuse.

◈ Bonus: Weekly Reflection Prompts

Every Friday, ask your AI:

"What did I learn this week? What systems are working? Where am I still doing things manually? What can I automate, clarify, or outsource next?"

Document it. Watch your progress compound.

This isn't a sprint to become an AI nerd.

It's a 30-day reboot to become dangerously capable in a world where most people still think prompting is cheating.

You now speak the language.

You have the tools.

You have the map.

Setting Up Your AI Toolkit: Plug-and-Play Recommendations

You don't need 100 tools.

You need a lean, powerful stack that fits your brain, your work, and your ambitions.

Here's your AI toolkit — plug-and-play style — grouped by purpose, not hype.

◈ Thinking, Writing, Prompting

ChatGPT (Pro): For drafting, summarizing, outlining, rewriting, and building custom GPTs

Claude (Anthropic): For deep reasoning, long documents, and philosophical clarity

Notion AI: For writing and organizing inside your second brain

Copy.ai or Jasper: For content marketers who want fast, multi-format generation

Use this stack when you want to:

Get from idea to draft in 5 minutes, without sounding like a sales bot.

◈ Automation & Workflow

Zapier: Easiest no-code connector between apps

Make: Visual workflows, more control, better for power users

Tally or Typeform: For forms that trigger automations

ChatGPT (code interpreter): For file handling, CSV magic, and mini automations

Use this stack when you want to:

Replace 5 steps with 1 click and never touch a spreadsheet again.

◈ Learning & Research

Perplexity.ai: Google, but faster, smarter, and source-backed

Glasp or Eightify: Summarize YouTube videos instantly

ChatGPT + PDF upload plugin: Turn dense PDFs into snackable insight

Anki: Build flashcards to actually retain what you learn

Use this stack when you want to:

Compress 10 hours of content into 30 minutes of usable knowledge.

◈ Content Creation & Branding

Midjourney: For stunning AI-generated art (via Discord)

DALL·E (in ChatGPT): For precise image editing and layout

Canva: Still king for fast visual content (templates + AI help)

ElevenLabs: For AI voiceovers that don't sound like robots

Descript: Edit podcasts and videos by editing the transcript

Use this stack when you want to:

Make professional content with zero production team.

◈ Personal OS / Second Brain

Notion: All-in-one task manager, planner, knowledge base

Mem.ai: Smart note-taking with automatic idea resurfacing

Reflect.app: For journaling, notes, and insights synced with your calendar

Rewind.ai (Mac only): Records everything on your screen — searchable memory

Use this stack when you want to:

Build a second brain that remembers, organizes, and reflects with you.

◈ Privacy & Sovereignty Tools

Brave or Arc browser: For privacy-first web browsing

PrivateGPT / Local LLMs: Run AI models on your own device

ProtonMail / Tutanota: For secure communication

Signal: For encrypted messaging

Obsidian: Offline, markdown-based personal knowledge base

Use this stack when you want to:

Use AI without giving your entire life to the cloud.

◈◈ Start Lean. Scale Smart.

You don't need all of these to start.

Pick one from each lane:

Writing → ChatGPT

Automation → Zapier

Content → Midjourney or Canva

Thinking → Notion

Learning → Perplexity

Privacy → Brave

Use them daily. Get weird. Break things. Rebuild better.

This is your AI armory.

You're no longer just "keeping up."

You're building a system that makes you faster, sharper, and harder to replace.

13

Conclusion

You Are Now Superhuman (If You Use It Right)

    You made it.

You didn't just read about AI.

You learned how to live with it. Create with it. Think with it. Leverage it.

Most people will never do that.

Most people will wait to be told what's safe. What's ethical. What's "best practice."

They'll use AI the way they use email: reactively, passively, with low expectations and no imagination.

But not you.

Because now you know:

- How to write, learn, plan, and build faster than ever
- How to see through the noise, filter the BS, and protect your mind
- How to turn AI into a second brain, a creative sidekick, and a productivity machine
- How to stay human while using machines to your advantage

You're not going to get replaced.

You're going to get dangerously efficient — and undeniably valuable.

And maybe even a little scary (in the good way).

From here on out, every task, idea, and ambition you touch can be amplified.

Not by working harder. But by working like someone who knows how to wield modern tools without becoming a tool.

You're not falling behind. You're designing your own upgrade path. Welcome to Human 2.0.

Bonus: 50 Prompts That Will Change Your Life
These are plug-and-play, category-sorted, ready to go. Copy, paste, modify, repeat.

◇ Productivity & Planning
• "Plan my week around these goals. Show me one priority per day."
• "Turn this to-do list into categories: deep work, admin, urgent, optional."
• "Build me a minimalist morning routine based on my energy patterns."
• "I'm overwhelmed. Ask me 5 questions to help clarify what I need to do next."
• "Summarize the 3 things I should focus on this month based on this journal entry."

◇ Writing & Communication
• "Write a polite but firm email asking for overdue payment."
• "Turn this paragraph into a LinkedIn post with a strong hook."
• "Give me 5 subject line options that feel personal and click-worthy."
• "Make this feedback sound encouraging but direct."
• "Rewrite this to sound like a confident, no-BS founder."

◇ Creativity & Brainstorming
• "List 10 wild ideas for a business that combines AI + nature + storytelling."
• "Help me brainstorm podcast episode titles that don't sound boring."
• "Give me 5 analogies for 'imposter syndrome' that I could turn into content."
• "What are 3 unconventional ways to grow a newsletter audience?"

- "Turn this shower thought into a tweet thread."

◈ Learning & Study
- "Break down this article into 5 flashcards with Q&A format."
- "Create a 7-day crash course on modern stoicism using free resources."
- "What's the opposite of this idea? Help me explore it."
- "Test me on this material with 10 multiple choice questions."
- "Explain this concept like I'm 12... and again like I'm Elon Musk."

◈ AI Mastery & Prompting
- "Show me 3 ways to improve this prompt for better output."
- "Compare Claude, ChatGPT, and Perplexity for writing a blog post."
- "What are the hidden limitations of GPT-4-turbo I should know?"
- "Generate a prompt that helps me build a personal assistant bot."
- "Help me teach others how to prompt like a pro using examples."

◈ Mindset, Motivation, Reflection
- "I'm feeling stuck. Give me a 3-step reset ritual."
- "Turn this venting session into a lesson I can share with others."
- "Summarize what I've learned this month — and what I'm avoiding."
- "What would future me thank me for doing this week?"
- "What belief am I holding right now that might be holding me back?"

◈ Business, Brand, and Side Hustles
- "Write a landing page for my [product/service] using AIDA structure."
- "Give me a launch plan for my new newsletter — 30 days, no ads."
- "Build a content strategy based on these 3 audience pain points."
- "List 10 digital product ideas I can build in a weekend using AI."

- "Position me as a thought leader without sounding like a douchebag."

One prompt per day = 50 days of leverage.
Use them. Tweak them. Share them.
Most people will scroll past. You'll ship.

Final Reminder:
You don't need to become a machine.
You just need to build one that works for you.

THE END

14

BONUS SECTION: Copy-Paste Your Way to Glory

B ONUS SECTION: Copy-Paste Your Way to Glory

50 Life-Changing Prompts

◈ Career Growth (8 Prompts)

1. "Rewrite my résumé summary to sound bold, strategic, and like someone who gets hired fast."

2. "Generate 5 strong bullet points for this job experience that focus on outcomes, not duties."

3. "Based on this job post and my experience, write a punchy, confident cover letter."

4. "List 10 unique value propositions I bring to the table that AI can't replace."

5. "What are 5 overlooked skills I could add to my resume to future-proof my role?"

6. "Generate 3 killer elevator pitches for me based on my career history and personality."

7. "How would I pitch myself as a consultant or fractional executive in my current industry?"

8. "Help me write a one-page personal manifesto for my career values and future direction."

◈ Side Hustle Launch (8 Prompts)

9.   "Give me 10 side hustle ideas that combine my skills in [X] and my obsession with [Y]."

10.   "Write a one-page landing page for a productized service I could offer solo."

11.   "Turn this idea into a 30-day launch plan using only free tools and AI support."

12.   "Write 3 cold outreach emails to test interest in this idea — casual, curious, not pushy."

13.   "Outline a $99 product I could create and sell by next month using existing content."

14.   "Give me a business model for a paid community built around [specific niche]."

15.   "What's a high-leverage lead magnet I could make in a weekend to grow a list?"

16.   "Help me write a personal brand bio that makes me sound like a magnetic weirdo people want to follow."

◈ Creativity & Content (8 Prompts)

17.   "Outline a 5-part email series for people struggling with burnout in creative work."

18.   "Write 5 tweet-length hot takes about AI and the future of work."

19.   "Give me 3 weird metaphors to explain procrastination like it's a villain in a comic book."

20.   "Help me brainstorm a content pillar strategy for my brand with 3 core themes."

21.   "Turn this article into: 1 tweet thread, 1 IG caption, 1 newsletter hook, 1 YouTube title."

22.   "Write a YouTube video script in the tone of [insert person or brand] about [topic]."

23.   "List 10 idea starters for short-form videos that combine humor + insight in my niche."

24.   "Write a CTA that doesn't sound like every other annoying content bro."

◈ Learning & Memory (8 Prompts)

25.   "Break this article into 10 flashcards with spaced repetition-style Q&A."

26.   "Give me a 30-day self-study plan to learn [topic] in 20 minutes a day."

27.   "Test me on this topic with a 10-question quiz — mix formats and add explanations."

28.   "Turn this video transcript into a learning guide with summaries and reflection questions."

29.   "Summarize this dense topic in 5 bullet points, a metaphor, and a real-world example."

30.   "Build a study schedule that balances review, practice, and note consolidation for retention."

31.   "What are the 5 most common misunderstandings about this concept?"

32.   "Make me a 7-day challenge to master the fundamentals of [topic] with daily AI prompts."

◈ Therapy, Coaching & Confidence Building (9 Prompts)

33.   "Ask me 5 hard questions that will help uncover why I keep sabotaging progress."

34.   "Reframe this negative belief in 3 different empowering ways. Be real, not corny."

35.   "Write a pep talk to myself as if I were my own future self who already figured it out."

36.   "Help me identify 3 blind spots in how I talk about my goals or identity."

37.   "I'm feeling stuck. Give me a journaling prompt to help process this without spiraling."

38.   "Write an affirmation that doesn't feel like toxic positivity but still

motivates me."

39. "List 10 things I've done in the last year that prove I'm not falling behind."

40. "Simulate a coaching session where you challenge my current excuses around [topic]."

41. "I'm afraid of success. Help me unpack why that fear feels safer than action."

◈ Planning, Productivity & Lifestyle Hacks (9 Prompts)

42. "Take this mess of tasks and organize them into a weekly plan I can actually follow."

43. "Write a simple morning routine that primes me for creative focus without overwhelming me."

44. "What's one habit I could automate or eliminate to reclaim 5 hours a week?"

45. "Build me a Notion page structure for life planning, task tracking, and creative work."

46. "Turn this weekly to-do list into categories: needle-movers, admin, avoid-if-possible."

47. "What does my perfect 'lazy productive' Sunday look like if I want to reset but not hustle?"

48. "Generate a quarterly planning ritual that combines reflection, goal-setting, and scheduling."

49. "Write a list of rules or heuristics I can use to say no more often without guilt."

50. "Create a frictionless daily check-in prompt that helps me track energy, mood, and focus."

Use one a day. Remix them. Share them. Build your playbook.

This is how you go from overwhelmed consumer...

to augmented creator.